# THE LORD'S PRAYER

ALSO BY WILLIAM BARCLAY IN THIS SERIES

*The Ten Commandments*

*The Parables of Jesus*

*The Apostles' Creed*

*We Have Seen the Lord!*

*At the Last Trumpet*

*Good Tidings of Great Joy*

*Discovering Jesus*

*Growing in Christian Faith*

*The New Testament*

*Barclay's Life of Jesus*

*New Testament Words*

# The Lord's Prayer

## WILLIAM BARCLAY

WESTMINSTER JOHN KNOX PRESS

LOUISVILLE, KENTUCKY

© The Estate of William Barclay, 1964, 1998

Originally published in 1964 as
*The Plain Man looks at the Lord's Prayer*

First published in this edition in 1998 by

ARTHUR JAMES LTD
Berkhamsted, Hertfordshire, England

Published in the U.S.A. in 1998 by

WESTMINSTER JOHN KNOX PRESS
Louisville, Kentucky

Typesetting by Strathmore Publishing Services, London
Cover design by Jennifer Cox

Printed in Singapore
00  01  02  03  04  05  06  07 – 10  9  8  7  6  5  4  3  2

A catalog card for this book may be obtained from the
Library of Congress

ISBN 0-664-25815-8

IN MEMORY OF MY CHIEF

G. H. C. M.

A MAN OF PRAYER

# Contents

# Foreword

*by the Archbishop of Canterbury*

Whether in his volumes for *The Daily Study Bible*, or in his other works, William Barclay achieved a balance between fine scholarship and popular exposition, which few others have achieved this century. Throughout my own ministry I have found myself turning to his works time and again for clarification of the classical or biblical background to an incident in the New Testament, or for a story that would bring to life the teaching lying behind a complex passage in one of Paul's Epistles.

I am delighted, therefore, that not only does *The Daily Study Bible* remain in print but that steps have now been taken to re publish these volumes from the series originally titled 'The Plain Man's Guides'. I am quite convinced that each of them still has a great deal to teach a new generation of Bible students, whether lay or ordained, both in what they say and in how they say it.

My hope, then, is that through this re-publication of several of Dr Barclay's works many of our contemporaries will discover the power of the Gospel which inspired him, and – which was his great longing behind everything he wrote – that they should discover for themselves the greatness of the Master.

† George Cantuar

*Lambeth Palace*
March 1998

ix

# Preface

This book was first published in 1964 and is the second in a series originally titled 'The Plain Man's Guides', which also includes *The Beatitudes*, *The Apostles' Creed* and *The Ten Commandments (Ethics)*. My father once described himself as a 'middle man', passing on the results of study and scholarship to 'the ordinary man and woman'. It was his aim to use simple language, remove jargon and allow everyone to understand the meaning and message of the New Testament. The contents of this book appeared originally in the *Preacher's Quarterly*.

William Barclay's aim is to remind people of what they are doing when they pray the Lord's Prayer, to make them think about its meaning and purpose and to do this in such a way as to make it relevant and up-to-date. He wants us to become more and more conscious of God's fatherly love and care for us. Jesus has given us a prayer which is a prayer to use by itself and a pattern for all prayer. Because of our familiarity with the Lord's Prayer it has perhaps become a string of meaningless words and this book shows us the depth in each phrase and leads us to a fuller understanding of those words we say so often.

'And so, when we have prayed the Lord's Prayer we rise from our knees and go out to the world and its ways remembering the royal sovereignty of God,... remembering the dynamic power of God,... remembering the glory of God.' If this book makes you think a little more each time you say the words of this beautiful prayer and encourages you to act in accordance with these words, then it will have achieved my father's aim.

RONALD W. BARCLAY
*Bedford*, March 1998

# Introduction

*What will I say?*

Often, when we had a letter to write when we were very young, we would go to our parents or to some older person and ask: 'What will I say?' And many of us, perhaps indeed most of us, remain like that all our lives. In the East the letter-writer was a professional figure. There he sat with his little desk and his pot of ink and his pen, and, if anyone wanted a letter written, it was to the letter-writer that he went. People needed someone to tell them what to say. In our countries we can go into a shop and buy a manual of letter-writing, a handbook which will give us specimen letters to show us what to say on different occasions.

When we ask: 'What will I say?' we do not really mean quite that. We know quite well what we want to say. We may want to send a word of thanks for a gift or for a kindness; we may want to send a request for help or for information; we may want to send a message of friendship or good-will or love; we may want to send our good wishes or our sympathy or our congratulations or even our complaints. This much we know. The problem that most people have is not to know *what* to say but to know *how* to say it. Very few people are really articulate; most people have real difficulty in putting their thoughts into words, and still more difficulty in putting their feelings into words.

If a person who wants to know: 'What will I say?' goes to someone and asks that question, it is not much help to be given the answer; 'Oh, just sit down and write.' This is exactly what the person cannot do. This is precisely his problem. He wants to know how he can get down on paper and into words the things he knows he ought to say. It is the same with making a speech. Often someone who has to make a speech at a wedding reception or at some other such function will go to someone who is good at making speeches and say: 'I've got to make a speech at a wedding. Tell me what to say.' He knows quite well that he wants to convey his own and other people's good wishes and kind thoughts and congratulations, but his problem is how to do it and how to set about it, and it is not much help to him to say: 'Just get up and talk.' If he could do that, he would not be asking for help.

When a person comes with this request, 'What will I say?' there are two ways in which he can be given help. The person helping can simply dictate the letter or the speech for him to write down, or can write it out for him to copy. That is one way to help, but it is not the best way to help, for if help is given in that way, the letter will be someone else's letter, and the speech will be someone else's speech. It will no doubt say all the right and the necessary things, but it may well say them in a way and in a style that the person who needed the help would never have used himself. The personal and the individual touch will be quite lacking.

But there is another way to help. The person needing help may be given, not a dictated letter or speech to repeat and to copy without alteration, but rather an outline and a pattern, which will be a guide through which he is enabled to express things in his own way. This is far the better way, for in this way the person is enabled to say the right things, but to say them in his own way.

It is exactly this that happened with Jesus and his disciples in regard to prayer. They wanted to pray; they knew their own needs and desires; they knew that God could satisfy them; but they really did not know how to set about praying. 'Lord,' they said, 'teach us to pray' (Luke 11.1). 'When you pray,' said Jesus, 'pray like this,' and he taught them the Lord's Prayer (Luke 11.2; Matthew 6.9). But what he was doing was that he was giving them a pattern of prayer far more than a form of words which they were to do no more than repeat, like children reciting a lesson.

The experience of the disciples is the experience of very many of us. We wish to pray for we know well that we need God. But we hardly know how to start; and we do not know how to put it. And Jesus, just as he gave it to his disciples, gives us in the Lord's Prayer, not only a prayer to repeat in itself, but a prayer to be for us the pattern of our own prayers.

And the pattern is very simple but very comprehensive. In the Lord's Prayer Jesus says to us:

When you pray,

> Remember that God is your Father and your King, and that, therefore, you go to One in whom Love and Power are equally combined.

When you pray,

> Do not hesitate to tell God about your daily needs.

When you pray,

> Do not shrink from telling God about your mistakes.

When you pray,

> Never forget to place the unknown future and all its perils in the hands of God.

In the Lord's Prayer in answer to his disciples' request Jesus gave to them and gave to us a prayer which is at one and the same time a prayer to use by itself and a pattern for all prayer.

# CHAPTER ONE

# A Praying People

There could be nothing more natural than that one of Jesus' disciples should come to him and ask him to teach them how to pray (Luke 11.1), for the Jews were characteristically and pre-eminently a praying people.

They came to God with an absolute confidence that God desired their prayers and that God would hear. 'The Holy One', said the rabbis, 'yearns for the prayers of the righteous.' 'The Lord is near to all who call upon him,' said the Psalmist, 'to all who call upon him in truth' (Psalm 145.18). 'They cried to the Lord in their trouble, and he delivered them from their distress' (Psalm 107.6). 'When he calls to me,' says God of the good man, 'I will answer him' (Psalm 91.15). For that reason we will do well to see the Jewish heritage of prayer into which the disciples had entered before they ever received the teaching and the example of Jesus.

No Jew ever doubted the power of prayer. 'Prayer, the weapon of the mouth,' said the rabbis, 'is mighty.'[1] No Jew ever doubted that God's ear and heart were open to the prayer of all his children. 'All are equal when they pray before God, women and slaves, sage and simpleton, poor and rich.'[2] Though all the world should pray at once, God will hear the prayer of each one. They quoted the verse, 'O thou that hearest prayer, unto thee shall all

1 Tanh. Beshallah 9. f. iiia.
2 Quoted I. Abrahams: *Studies in Pharisaism and the Gospels*, Second Series, 82.

flesh come' (Psalm 65.2). Then they went on to say: 'A human
king can hearken to two or three people at once, but he cannot
hearken to more; God is not so, for all men may pray to him, and
he hearkens to them all simultaneously. Men's ears become
satisfied with hearing; but God's ears are never satiated. He is
never wearied by men's prayers.'[3] Nor is God ever bored by the
continual coming of his children. There is a rabbinic parable: 'A
man visits his friend and his friend greets him cordially, placing
him on the couch beside him. He comes again, and is given a
chair. He comes again and receives a stool. He comes a fourth
time and the friend says, "The stool is too far off, I cannot fetch it
for you." But God is not so. For whenever Israel knocks at the
door of God's house, the Holy One rejoices, as it is written; For
what great nation is there that hath a God so nigh unto them as
our God is, *whenever* we call?'[4] To a man a friend may be less and
less welcome on each visit, until he becomes a nuisance, but it is
never so with God.

Once the Temple had been destroyed in AD 70, and once
sacrifice became for ever impossible for the Jew, prayer became
the supreme sacrifice and offering; but even before that there
were many rabbis who would have held that prayer is greater in
the sight of God than sacrifice. 'God said to Israel, Be assiduous
in regard to devotion, for there is no finer quality than prayer.
Prayer is greater than all the sacrifices.'[5] 'In the law of the
sacrifices it says, If a man has a bullock let him offer a bullock; if
not, let him give a ram, or a lamb, or a pigeon; and if he cannot
afford a pigeon, let him bring a handful of flour. And if he has not
even any flour, let him bring nothing at all, but come with words
of prayer.'[6]

---

3 *Midrash* on Psalm 65.
4 *Midrash* on Psalm 4: *T. B. Yoma* 76a.
5 Isaiah 1.11, 13: Tanh. Wayera I, f 31b.
6 Hosea 14.2: Tanh. B. Zaw, viii, 9a.

As the Jewish teachers saw it, prayer should be constant, and not simply when a man is in need. The Talmud uses as an illustration the saying in Ecclesiasticus, 'Honour the physician *before* you have need of him,' and goes on to comment: 'The Holy One says, Just as it is my office to cause the rain and the dew to fall, and make the plants to grow to sustain man, so art thou bounden to pray before me, and to praise me in accordance with my works; thou shalt not say, I am in prosperity, wherefore shall I pray? But when misfortune befalls me then will I come and supplicate. Before misfortune comes, anticipate and pray.'[7] Prayer is not so much an emergency appeal in need as it is a continuing and unbroken conversation and fellowship with God.

Friedländer very beautifully sets out the feelings in the heart which lead a man to pray.[8] We ought to take everything that is in our hearts and lay it before God. By that very fact we are compelled to examine the desires of our hearts, to see whether they contain anything that is unholy, unjust or ignoble. 'Prayer has the salutary effect of purifying, refining, and ennobling our heart. It banishes evil thoughts, and thus saves us much pain and sorrow.'[9] Let us then see, as Friedländer put it for his people, the feelings of the heart which we should bring to God.

We should bring our *love*. 'I will bless the Lord at all times: his praise shall continually be in my mouth' (Psalm 34.2). 'O Lord, open my lips; and my mouth shall show forth thy praise' (Psalm 51.17). Clearly, we should bring our *gratitude* and our *thanksgiving*. 'I will praise thee, for thou hast heard me' (Psalm 118.21). 'I will sacrifice unto thee with the voice of thanksgiving' (Jonah 2.9). As one of the rabbis had it: 'Though all prayers were to be discontinued, prayers of thanksgiving will never be discontinued.'

---

7 Ecclesiasticus 33.31: Exod. R. ch. xxiii.
8 M. Friedländer, *The Jewish Religion*, 280–284.
9 M. Friedländer, *The Jewish Religion*, 183.

And yet we must have a care that we thank God for the right things. 'When thy enemy falls, do not rejoice.' The Talmud has a very lovely passage: 'The Angels wished to sing praises to God while the Egyptians were drowning in the sea, and God rebuked them saying, Shall I listen to your hymns when my children are perishing before my eyes ?'[10] As the Jewish teachers saw it, no man can ever give God thanks for the misfortune of any other man. Always when a man prays he must have in his mind the *holiness* of God. However much a man comes to God in love and in trust and in confidence, there must still be that reverence which will prevent an undue familiarity on the part of the creature before his Creator. 'In his prayer,' said Rabbi Simon, 'a man should think that the Shechinah (i.e. the glory of God) is before him.'[11]

When a man has in his mind the holiness of God, as he prays, there must of necessity be two other things in his mind. There must be *the desire to obey and to please God.* 'How sweet are thy words to my taste,' said the Psalmist, 'sweeter than honey to my mouth!' 'My tongue will sing of thy word, for all thy commandments are right' (Psalm 119.103, 172). There will be *the fear to offend God.* It is only the man with clean hands and a pure heart who can ascend into the hill of the Lord (Psalm 24.3, 4). It is the Psalmist's determination: 'I will wash mine hands in innocence, and go about thine altar, O Lord' (Psalm 26.6). Above all, in prayer a man will take all his weakness to the strength of God. A man is only too well aware of the insecurity of life, of his helplessness in face of the chances and the changes of life, of the way in which the light can suddenly turn to darkness. 'The Lord,' said the Psalmist, 'is a stronghold for the oppressed, a stronghold in time of trouble' (Psalm 9.9). As the Talmud had it: 'Even when the edge of the sword already touches a man's neck, even then he must not

---

10 T. B. Yebamoth 64a.                    11 San. 22a.

abandon his faith in praying to God.'[12] 'Hope in the Lord and pray again.'[13]

There are still other things which we must note about the Jewish idea of prayer that we may see still more clearly the heritage which the disciples already possessed before Jesus taught them to pray.

A great part of prayer was *penitence*. 'The gate of tears is never shut.'[14] Even if the congregation can bring nothing else, they can weep and pray and God will receive them.[15] To the prayer of penitence the Jews attribute a quite extraordinary power. The Jew was always fascinated by what we may call the paradox of God. The decrees of God are immutable; his laws are inviolable; his judgements are inevitable. It would, therefore, seem that God's condemnation of the sinner is quite unalterable. And yet the fact remains true that there is such a thing as the wonder of the mercy of God. The Jew literally believed that the prayer of the penitent heart could turn the wrath of God into the mercy of God. 'Why is the prayer of the righteous like a rake? As the rake turns the grain from place to place, so the prayer of the righteous turns the attribute of mercy.'[16] Rabbi Ishmael once when he was acting as a priest entered into the innermost sanctuary to burn incense. There he saw God, and prayed to God, 'May it be thy will that thy mercy subdue thy wrath,' and God nodded in assent.[17] Perhaps the most astonishing picture in all Jewish religious writing is the picture of God praying to himself that his mercy may prevail. Rab said that the prayer of God ran thus: 'May it be my will that my compassion may overcome mine anger, and that it may prevail over my attributes of justice and judgement, and that I may deal with my children according to the attribute of compassion, and

12 T. B. Ber. 5a.
13 R. Deut. ii.
14 T. B. Ber. 32b.
15 R. Exod. xxviii. 4.
16 Yeb. 64a.
17 T. B. Ber. 7a.

that I may not act towards them according to the strict line of justice.'[18] Israel Abrahams quotes the line of Solomon Ibn Gabirol in his *Royal Crown*, 'the most inspired hymn after the Psalter': 'From thee I fly to thee.'[19] Surely this is the most vivid of all ways of saying that it did not cost God nothing to forgive sin.

The highest prayer is always *the prayer of the community*. The prayer of an individual always tends to be, or runs the risk of being, selfish; and, therefore, the highest kind of prayer is the prayer of the community, from which a man must never separate himself. 'Israel will be redeemed only when it forms one single band: when all are united they will receive the presence of the Shechinah.'[20] It is only that man who shares in the troubles of the community, as Moses shared in the distresses of his brethren, who will see the consolation of the community.[21] When the righteous are even on the point of death they do not think of their own concerns but of the needs of the community. When Moses was told that he must die (Numbers 27.12–14), his immediate concern was not for himself, but that God should appoint another leader in his place.[22] Perhaps the most extraordinary instance of this line of thought is in the curious rabbinic prayer: 'Let not the prayer of wayfarers find entrance, O Lord, before thee.'[23] The idea is that the wayfarer might be asking for fine weather when the country as a whole needed rain. It is not that Jewish thought either condemned or neglected personal and private prayer, far from it; it is simply that the Jew had a horror of selfishness in prayer, and, therefore, stressed the need of praying in and with the community, and we may well remember that the words *I*, *me*, *my*, and *mine* never appear in the Lord's Prayer.

18 Ber. 7a.
19 I. Abrahams, *Studies in Pharisaism and the Gospels*, Second Series, 90.
20 Aboth 2.5.                       21 Ta'an. IIa.
22 Sifre Num. Pinehas 138f. 52a.    23 T. Jer. Joma 5.2.

The Jew strongly believed in *perseverance* in prayer. Moses still prayed for the mercy of God, even when God said to him, 'Enough for thee, speak no more to me of this matter!' (Deuteronomy 3.26). How much less should other men desist when their prayer is not answered! After the sin of the golden calf Moses interceded for Israel for forty days (Deuteronomy 9.18, 25). The rabbis tell how Hezekiah in his mortal illness did not give up praying even when Isaiah announced to him in the name of the Lord that he must die and not live (Isaiah 38.1-5). We have a family tradition, he said to the prophet, that even if a sharp sword is resting on a man's throat, he should not refrain from craving mercy.[24] Prayer, repentance and almsgiving are the three things which can cause even a decree of God to be rescinded.[25] The Jew saw nothing wrong and nothing unnatural in pleading with God.

Although prayer must be offered in perseverance and in persistence, it must nonetheless be offered in *humility*. Always the person who prayed made it clear that he wanted nothing other than the will of God. 'May it be thy good pleasure to grant …'; 'what is good in thine eyes, do,' are the standard beginnings for prayer. 'Learn to say, Whatever the Almighty does is done for our good.'[26] No man must pray and expect an answer as a right. A haughty prayer is an abomination. There is a curious saying: 'To three sins man is daily liable, thoughts of evil, *reliance on prayer*, and slander. He who prays thinking he deserves an answer, receives none.'[27] The idea is that there can be a confidence in prayer which is an arrogant supposition that God must do what those who pray ask. An answer to prayer is always a boon and never a right. 'Do not make thy prayer a fixed claim or demand, which must be

24 Sifre Deut. 29; Ber. 10a.          25 Jer. Ta'an. 65b; Jer. Sanh. 28c.
26 Ber. 60b.
27 Ber. 32b; 55a; Baba Bathra 164b; Rosh Hashanah 18a.

fulfilled, but a supplication for mercy which may or may not be granted.'[28] Even in prayer a man must remember that God is the Creator and that he is the created.

To the Jew *intercession* was specially precious. It is a prayer which is uttered on behalf of another which is always answered first.[29] Rab said: 'Whoever has it in his power to pray on behalf of his neighbour, and fails to do so, is called a sinner.'[30] Here is another instance of the Jewish horror of being selfish in prayer. It is at least as important to pray for others as it is to pray for oneself.

Just because prayer held so high a place in Jewish thought and life, it was specially liable to certain dangers and to certain misuses, dangers and misuses which were much in Jesus' mind when he spoke to his disciples about prayers. The one supreme danger was the danger of *formalism*. Just because the Jews were so anxious to see that prayer was never omitted, that it was given its proper place in life, the tendency was to surround it with rules and regulations. And yet very many writers are quite unfair to the Jews in dealing with this matter for two reasons. First, such formalism as there was sprang entirely from the determination and the desire to give prayer its proper place in life. Second, there was no one more aware of the dangers than the Jews themselves, and in their finest thought they lay down the very laws by which the formalism can be overcome, and by which in so many cases it was overcome. Schürer writes: 'Even prayer itself, that centre of religious life, was bound in the fetters of a rigid mechanism.'[31] There is truth there, but it is only half the truth, and we will go on to look at the dangers, but we will not forget the ideals behind them, for, as Aristotle said long ago, any person or any institution must be judged by his and its best and highest manifestation.

---

28 Aboth. 2.13.                    29 Baba Quama 92a.
30 Ber. 12b.
31 E. Schürer: *History of the Jewish People in the Time of Christ*, 2.2. 115.

(i) There was formalism in regard to *time*. The devout Jew prayed three times a day, at 9 a.m., at 12 noon, and at 3 p.m. With the characteristic Jewish desire to trace things as far back as possible, the morning prayer was ascribed to Abraham (Genesis 19.27); the afternoon prayer to Isaac (Genesis 24.63); and the evening service to Jacob (Genesis 28.11). Daniel, too, prayed three times a day looking toward Jerusalem (Daniel 6.10). It is quite true that this could become a sheer formalism, and that it could become an opportunity for ostentation, for, wherever a man was at the hours of prayer, he prayed, and he might well deliberately choose a place where as many as possible might see him. David, too, said, 'At evening, at morning, and at noon, will I pray and cry aloud' (Psalm 55.17). This could, of course, become a ritual prayer cycle; but it is also true that the devout Jew could say: 'Would that man were capable of praying continuously, all day long!'[32]

(ii) There was formalism in regard to *place*. Just as a man had to pray at the right time, so also he had to pray in the right place. Abba Benjamin said: 'A man's prayer is only heard by God when offered in a Synagogue.'[33] Rabbi Huna said: 'Who ever fixes a place for prayer, has the God of Abraham for his help.'[34] Rabbi Jochanan said that a man should have a place exclusively kept for prayer.[35] Peter and John were going up to the Temple at three o'clock in the afternoon 'at the hour of prayer' when they came upon the lame man at the Beautiful Gate and healed him (Acts 3.1). But it would be very wrong to take that as the only rule of Jewish prayer. This very same Rabbi Jochanan said that the man who prays in his house surrounds it with a wall of iron[36] – which is one of the loveliest things ever said about family worship.

---

32 Tan. B., Mikkez 98a–98b.
34 Ber. 6b.
36 Jer. Ber. 8d.

33 Ber. 6a.
35 Jer. Ber. 8b.

And there is a Midrash on one of the Psalms which says: 'God says to Israel: Pray in the Synagogue of your city; if you cannot, pray in the field; if you cannot, pray in your house; if you cannot, pray on your bed; if you cannot, commune with your own heart upon your bed and be still.'[37] There is nowhere where God cannot be found. Even if a working man was working on the top of a tree, or on a scaffolding against a building, it was permitted to pray at the hour of prayer just where he was.[38] In any Synagogue it was the rule to pray facing towards Jerusalem, and in the Temple it was the rule to pray facing the Holy of Holies; and yet at the same time it must be remembered that the rabbis could say: 'A blind man, or one who is unable to locate the directions should direct his heart to his Father in Heaven.'[39] True, there could be formalism in regard to place but beyond the formalism there was the certainty that God does not dwell in any Temple made with hands.

(iii) There was formalism in regard to the *set forms* of prayer. The greatest of all Jewish prayers is the *Shemoneh 'Esreh*, which means The Eighteen. It consisted of eighteen prayers in the form of benedictions, all with the phrase, 'Blessed be thou.' It was called the *Tefillah*, which means The Prayer, as it were, *par excellence*. It was part of every Jewish Synagogue service, and every devout Jew was to pray it three times a day. There was even an 'abstract' of it which might be used when a man could not pray the full prayer: 'Give us understanding, O Lord our God, to know thy ways; to circumcise our hearts, to fear thee, and forgive us so that we may be redeemed. Keep us far from sorrow. Satiate us on the pastures of thy land, and gather our scattered ones from the four corners of the earth. Let the righteous rejoice in the rebuilding of thy city and in the establishment of thy Temple,

37 Midrash Psalms iv. 9. 23b; Pesickta 158b.
38 M. Ber. 4.4.                          39 Ber. 30a.

and in the flourishing of the horn of David, thy servant, and in the clear-shining light of the son of Jesse, thine anointed. Even before we call, do thou answer. Blessed art thou, O Lord, who hearkenest unto prayer.'[40]

There were set prayers for all the events of life. These prayers are set out in the treatise in the Mishnah called *Berachoth*, which means Benedictions. At the sight of fruits, or wine, or vegetables, or any of the produce of the earth, a man should say: 'Blessed art thou who createst the fruit of the tree, the fruit of the vine, the fruit of the earth.' (6.1). If a man sees shooting stars, earthquakes, lightnings, thunders and storms, he should say: 'Blessed is he whose power and might fill the world.' When he sees mountains, hills, rivers, deserts, he should say: 'Blessed is the author of creation.' For rain and good tidings, he should say: 'Blessed is he, the good and the doer of good.' At bad tidings, he should say: 'Blessed is he, the true judge.' If he has built a house or acquired anything new he should say: 'Blessed is he who hath given us life.' A man should pray every time he enters and leaves a city (9.1–4). It is easy to see how such a custom and a ritual might well become a formality, and little more than a kind of use of magic incantations, but surely it is equally easy to see how a man who had such habits of prayer necessarily lived in a world which was full of God, a world in which there was nothing and no event which did not turn his heart to Almighty God, the Creator and the Sustainer of all life.

(iv) There was formality in regard to *length*, and Jesus did warn against 'much speaking' (Matthew 6.7). But the Jewish rabbinic teaching was very much on the side of Jesus. Rabbi Me'ir said: 'A man's words should always be few towards God.'[41] Rabbi Chijja ben Abba said: 'Whoever prolongs his prayer, and calculates on it

40 Ber. 29a.
41 Ber. 61a.

(that is, anticipates its fulfilment as a reward for its length), will eventually come to pain of heart.'[42]

In this the rabbis were very wise, for they held that there is a time to shorten and a time to lengthen. Thus in regard to Miriam, Moses prayed no more than, 'Lord, heal her,' (Numbers 12. 13), and yet Moses could also say, 'I worshipped before the Lord forty days and forty nights' (Deuteronomy 9.18).[43] The rabbis would have approved of long and ostentatious prayers no more than Jesus did. It is perfectly true that sometimes Jewish prayers pile up titles in address to God as the second section of the *Kaddish* does: 'Blessed, praised and glorified, exalted, extolled, honoured, magnified and lauded, be the name of the Holy One.' But the rabbinic teaching was that it was proper to apply three adjectives to God – great, mighty and revered.[44]

There are sayings on the other side: 'Whenever the righteous make their prayer long, their prayer is heard.'[45] 'Would that a man could pray all day long.'[46] But such sayings speak of the prayer of the loving heart, and of the man who continuously seeks the presence of God.

It is easy to make the charge of formalism against Jewish prayer. We may cite passages which declare that even a slip in the correct wording of a set prayer is fatal.[47] But there could hardly be anything more unfair, for formalism is the one thing which the great Jewish teachers sought with all their hearts to avoid.

The Jews described the first necessity of prayer by an almost untranslatable word. 'Prayer', they said, 'needs *kawannah*.'[48] *Kawannah* is concentrated intention and devotion; it is the attitude in which eyes and mind and heart are fixed on God. The demand for this attitude in prayer runs through all Jewish devotional

---

42 Ber. 32b.   43 Mechilta 29a.   44 Ber. 33b.

45 Yoma 29b.   46 Ber. 21a.   47 Ber. 5.5.

48 Jer. Ber. 7a.

thinking and writing. 'It matters not whether you do much or little, so long as your heart is directed to heaven.'[49] 'Everything depends on the *kawannah* of the heart.'[50] Even if a man is walking, he must stop to pray and 'direct his heart to God in awe and fear, trembling and quaking.'[51] Even the action of walking might deflect the thoughts and the intention of the heart. 'He who prays must direct his heart.'[52] Rab said: 'He whose mind is not quieted should not pray.' Rabbi Chanina was wont not to pray when he was irritated.[53] The Jew prayed standing with his hands stretched out, and Rabbi Ammi said: 'Man's prayer is not accepted unless he puts his heart in his hands.'[54] 'Let him who prays cast his eyes downwards, but turn his heart upwards.'[55] Rabbi Eleazar said: 'Always let a man test himself: if he can direct his heart, let him pray; if he cannot let him not pray.'[56]

Formalism was abhorrent to the devout Jew. 'Prayer should not be recited as if a man were reading a document'; and to avoid that, a new prayer should be said every day.[57] As soon as prayer becomes either a fixed task or a burden, it ceases to be prayer in any real sense of the term at all.[58]

The Mishnah lays it down that a man must not stand up to pray except in a serious state of mind,[59] and then the rabbis went on to say that a man should never come straight in from business or from a journey and pray, but that for an hour he ought to compose himself and his thoughts before he prays.

We may conclude our examination of the Jewish ideas of prayer by choosing out of very many three great Jewish prayers, which the Jews still pray, and which any Christian might take with profit upon his lips. First, there is a prayer for the night before sleeping:

49 Ber. 17a.

52 Ber. 3.6.

55 Yeb. 105b.

58 Ber. 29b.

50 Meg. 20a.

53 Erub. 65a.

56 Ber. 30b.

59 Ber. 5.1.

51 Tanh. Lek leak 24a.

54 Ta'an 8a.

57 J. Ber. 38a.

Blessed art thou, O Lord our God, King of the Universe, who makest the hands of sleep to fall upon mine eyes, and slumber upon mine eyelids. May it be thy will, O Lord my God, and God of my fathers, to suffer me to lie down in peace and to let me rise again in peace. Let not my thoughts trouble me, nor evil dreams, nor evil fancies, but let my rest be perfect before thee. O lighten mine eyes lest I sleep the sleep of death, for it is thou who givest light to the apple of the eye. Blessed art thou, O Lord, who givest light to the whole world in thy glory.[60]

Second, there is the prayer which Rabbi Yannai taught his disciples to pray when they woke in the morning:

Blessed art thou, O Lord, who quickenest the dead. May it be thy will, O Lord my God, to give me a good heart, a good nature, a good hope, a good eye, a good soul, a lowly soul, and a humble spirit; may thy name not be profaned among (or, through) us, and make us not a mockery in the mouth of men; may our end not be cut off, nor our hope be a vexation, and may we not need the gifts of flesh and blood, and put not our sustenance into their hands, for their gifts are small, and the shame they cause is great; and place our portion in thy Law, with those who do thy will; build up thy house, thy sanctuary, thy city, thy temple, speedily, in our days.[61]

Lastly, there is the prayer of Rab:

May it be thy will, O Lord our God, to grant us long life, a life of peace, a life of good, a life of blessing, a life of sustenance, a life of bodily vigour, a life marked by the fear of sin, a life free from shame and reproach, a life of prosperity and honour, and a life in which love of the Law and fear of heaven shall cling to us, a life wherein thou fulfillest the desire of the heart for good.[62]

---

60 Ber. 60b.          61 T. J. Ber. 7d.          62 Ber. 16b.

When Jesus' disciples came to him to ask him to teach them how and what to pray they came to him out of a priceless heritage of prayer, which through him was to become even greater and even more precious.

# CHAPTER TWO

# Our Father

Before we begin to study the petitions of the Lord's Prayer in detail we must stop to look at the general pattern of the prayer.

We cannot fail to see that the prayer begins by giving God his own and his proper place. The first three petitions of the prayer are for the hallowing of God's name, the coming of God's Kingdom, and the doing of God's will. It is only then that we turn to our own needs and our own requests. The great fault of prayer is that it can so easily become self-centred and self-seeking. We can be so busy thinking of what we want that we have no time to think of what God wants. We can be so concerned with our own desires that we never think of God's will. We can be so busy talking to God that we never give God the chance to talk to us. We can be so busy telling God that we never stop to listen to God.

It is precisely that kind of situation that the Lord's Prayer commands us and helps us to avoid. It begins by putting, not us, but God in the centre of the picture. The circumference can only be right when the centre is right. All other things can only take their proper place when God is given his proper place. The Lord's Prayer begins with the memory of the majesty of God, the memory of the purpose of God, and the acceptance of the will of God.

The second part of the prayer is the most comprehensive prayer that men were ever taught to pray. Let us set down its three petitions:

Give us this day our daily bread.

Forgive us our debts, as we forgive our debtors.

Lead us not into temptation, but deliver us from evil.

The first of these three petitions is a prayer for our *present* need. The second of them is a prayer for our *past* sin. The third of them is a prayer for our *future* welfare and goodness. These three short petitions take life, past, present and future, and lay it before God. Food for the present, forgiveness for the past, help for the future – all of life is brought into the presence of God.

But these three petitions do even more than that. When we pray the first of them, the prayer for daily bread, we think of *God the Father*, the creator and sustainer of all life. When we pray the second of them, the prayer for our forgiveness, we think of *God the Son*, the Saviour and Redeemer of all mankind and of us. When we pray the third of them, the prayer for future help to live without sin, we think of *God the Holy Spirit*, the Guide, the Helper and the Protector of all life. These three petitions bring us face to face with Father, Son and Holy Spirit. Within their narrow compass, and with their astonishing economy of words, these three brief petitions take the whole of life to the whole of God.

The pattern of the Lord's Prayer must be the pattern of all prayer, for it begins by giving God his proper place, and it goes on to take life's past, present and future to God, the Father, Son, and Holy Spirit.

Now we turn to the opening words of the Lord's Prayer, the words *Our Father*. It takes very much more than a dictionary to define the meaning of any word. To the definition of the dictionary there must be added the interpretation of experience. Of no word is that truer than of the word father. The word father has two quite distinct meanings. It can be used in the sense of *paternity*; in that sense it simply denotes the person who is

responsible for the birth of a child. In that case there is no necessary connection between the father and the child other than a
physical connection. A man may be the father of a child in the
paternity sense of the term, and never even set eyes on the child
for whose birth his action was responsible. But the word father
can be used in the sense of *fatherhood*. In that sense it describes a
relationship of love and intimacy and confidence and trust
between the father and the child. The Christian believes that God
is father in the paternity sense of the word, in the sense that it is
God who is the source of all life who gives life to any child but
the unique thing about the Christian idea of God is that the
Christian far more believes that God is father in the fatherhood
sense of the word, for he believes that between God and men
there is possible through Jesus Christ an intimate, lifelong, loving
relationship in which God and man come close together. This is
indeed a distinction which the Jewish teachers themselves made.

The rabbis told a story of an orphan girl who was brought up
by a good and faithful guardian. The day came when she was to
be married. The Scribe who was making the necessary legal
arrangements for the wedding asked her 'What is your name?'
And she told him. Then the Scribe asked: 'What is your father's
name?' The girl was silent. 'Why are you silent?' asked her
guardian. The girl answered: 'Because I know none other than
you as a father, for he who brings up is father, not he who begets.'
So, the rabbis said, the real father of Israel is not anyone who is
connected with Israel by any physical connection; it is God who
brought the nation up.

When we say to God, Our Father, it is not simply paternity
which is in our minds; it is the far closer relationship of fatherhood.

When Jesus taught his disciples to pray, Our Father, he was
speaking out of a rich heritage, for the fatherhood of God was a
conception that was supremely dear to a Jew. There were sayings

which were often upon Jewish lips. 'You are the sons of the Lord your God' (Deuteronomy 14.1). 'I am a father to Israel' (Jeremiah 31 .9). 'Is not he (the Lord) your father, who created you, who made you and established you?' (Deuteronomy 32.6). 'Yet, O Lord, thou art our father; we are the clay and thou art the potter; we are all the work of thy hand' (Isaiah 64.8). It was on texts like these that the loving devotion of the Jews fed itself. Their conviction of the fatherhood of God brought certain assurances to the Jews.

(i) Their belief in the fatherhood of God assured them of *the nearness of God*. Because God is father, the Jewish saints were sure that God is always near to hear and to answer prayer and to give his presence to his people. There is a Jewish interpretation of the instructions to Moses for the construction of the Tabernacle in Exodus 26.18–25. The *Shechinah* was the glory of God which sometimes settled on the Tabernacle and on the Temple in a luminous cloud. When God said to Moses: 'Make me a dwelling-place,' Moses wondered, for Moses well knew that the glory of God fills the upper and the lower worlds and he could not understand how the glory of God could dwell in a dwelling-place that he might be able to construct. But God spoke to Moses. 'Your thoughts', God said, 'are not my thoughts. Twenty boards to the north, and twenty to the south and eight to the west are enough for me (Exodus 26.18, 20, 25). And not only that, but I will come down and confine my Shechinah in one square yard..., You are the children of the Lord your God, and I am your Father (Deuteronomy 14.1; Jeremiah 31.9). It is an honour to children to be near their father, and an honour to a father to be near his children; therefore, make a house for the Father that he may dwell near his children' (Exod. R. Terumah xxxiv, 1, 3). God can confine his glory to one square yard. Just because God is Father and we are his children, even in the humblest home, even in the littlest and the barest church, even for the most unimportant person, the glory of God is there. Anywhere the Father can be and will be with his children.

The rabbis had another way of putting this. Rabbi Judah ben Simon said: 'An idol is near yet far; God is far yet near.' They asked him what he meant. 'An idolater makes an idol,' he said, 'and sets it up in his house. So the idol is near. But one may cry unto the idol and it will not answer, therefore the idol is far. But God is far yet near.' 'How?' they asked him. 'From here to heaven', he said, 'is a journey of five hundred years; therefore God is far; but he is also near, for, if a man prays and meditates in his heart, God is near to answer his prayer' (Deuteronomy R. Wa'ethanan 11.10). Even if the dwelling place of God is in the heights of heaven, even if heaven and earth cannot contain his dazzling glory, nevertheless because God is Father he is in the smallest and the humblest dwelling and near to the simplest heart.

(ii) The belief of the Jews in the fatherhood of God assured them of the *mercy of God* in judgement, and of his *willingness to accept the penitent heart*. Very beautifully it was said: 'God says to Israel: For all the wonders and mighty deeds which I have wrought for you, the only reward I ask is that you should honour me as my children, and call me your Father' (Exod. R. Mishpatim, xxxii. 5). The essence of God's relationship to men is fatherhood, and the dearest wish of God is that all his children should willingly enter into that relationship.

The Jewish saints thought of God as judge, but they thought of him as a judge who was also a father. There is a Jewish passage which tells of two men who came to the judgement seat in terror of the judge and who were told to take courage. 'So Israel will stand at the judgement before God, and will be afraid because of the Judge. Then the angels of the service will say to them: Fear not! Do you not recognize him? He is your fellow-citizen, as it is said, It is He who will build up my city (Isaiah 45.13). Then they will say: Fear not the Judge! Do you not recognize him? He is your kinsman, as it says, The children of Israel, the people related to Him (Psalm 148.14). Then they will say: Do you not recognize him? He is your brother, as it says, for my brethren and friends' sake (Psalm 122.8). And even more, He is your Father, as it is said, Is He not thy Father?' (Deuteronomy 32.6). Here is the beautiful thought that he who is judge is also fellow-citizen, kinsman, brother, and above all Father.

The conviction that God is Father made the Jewish saints quite sure that forgiveness was always open to the penitent heart. Just as the parent will forgive the child who comes and says, 'I'm sorry,' so will God. 'God says: I testify by heaven and earth that I sit and hope for Israel more than a father for his son or than a mother for her daughter, if only they would repent, so that my words could be fulfilled' (Tan.d.b. El. p.163). More than once the Jewish saints draw the picture of a prophet inviting the people to return in penitence to God, and of the people in the knowledge of their sin and their shame feeling the impossibility of even accepting the invitation. Then God says to them: 'If you come back to me, is it not to your Father in Heaven that you come back? As it is said, For I am a Father to Israel' (Jeremiah 31.9; Pes. K. 165a). There is another rabbinic passage about a king's son who ran away. The king sent his tutor to invite him to come back. 'With what face can I return?' said the son. 'I am ashamed before thee.' And the father answered: 'Can a son be ashamed to return to his father?' And even so it is with Israel and God (Deuteronomy R. Wa'ethanan 11.24). In passages like that there is a faith in God which comes very close to the conception of God in the parable of the Prodigal Son. Here is a picture of the God who is the Father, and whose only desire is that his wandering children should come home.

(iii) But in spite of the beauty of the Jewish idea of the fatherhood of God, the Jews never sentimentalized the idea. They were quite clear that the fatherhood of God involves the loving obedience of man. They were very definite that the idea of God as a loving father can never be used as an excuse for sinning; it must rather be the summons to holy obedience. When the prophets prayed to God to have mercy on his children, God answered: 'Only when they do my will are they my children; when they do not do my will they are not my children' (Exodus R. Ki Tissa xlvi, 4). 'Hearken', says the rabbinic passage, 'to thy Father who is in heaven. He deals with thee as with an only son, if thou obeyest him, but, if not, he deals with thee as a slave. When thou doest his will he is thy Father, and thou art his son, but if not, against thy will, and opposed to thy consent, he is thine owner and thou art his slave' (Pes. R. 132b).

Here is the idea that the will of God cannot in any event be gainsaid. He who willingly and obediently accepts it is the son of God; he who struggles against it has in the end to accept it, not as a loving son, but as a coerced slave, not as it were as a volunteer, but as a conscript. The Jewish saints allegorized the incident in Exodus 17.11 which tells how in the battle with Amalek Israel prevailed as long as Moses held up his hands but was defeated when Moses let his hands drop. 'But could the hands of Moses promote the battle or hinder the battle? It is rather to teach you that such time as the Israelites directed their thoughts on high, and kept their hearts in subjection to their Father in heaven, they prevailed; otherwise they suffered defeat' (Rosh ha-Shanah 3.8). In the same way it was not looking at the fiery serpent that cured the man bitten by the serpents; it was the directing of the eyes and the thoughts on high to God the Father. How can a man 'acquire God'? asks the Jewish preacher, and answers: 'He may acquire him by his good deeds and by the study of the law' (Tan.d.b. El. p.128). The duty of the teacher of children is to teach children 'to do the will of their Father who is in heaven.' Rabbi Judah, the son of Tema, gave the beautiful command: 'Be

strong as a leopard, light as an eagle, fleet as a hart, and strong as
a lion to do the will of thy Father who is in heaven' (Aboth v. 23).

The Jew always connected the thought of the loving and
gracious fatherhood of God not with any kind of licence to sin,
but with the absolute obligation to the response of loving
obedience.

(iv) We may note one last thing. The thought of the fatherhood of God laid upon the Jew the obligation to observe the
brotherhood of man. Rabbi Jose said: 'Why does God love
widows and orphans? Because their eyes are turned to him, as it
is said, A father of the fatherless, and a judge of the widows
(Psalm 68.5). Therefore, anyone who robs them is as if he robbed
God, their Father in heaven' (Exod. R. Mishpatim 30.8). If God is
Father, then God will never look lightly on the man who injures
or refuses to help one of his children.

Even before the Christian faith came into the world, and even
before Jesus taught his men to pray 'Our Father', there was in
Jewish thought a great heritage of riches in the Jewish connection
of the fatherhood of God. We now turn to study the new meaning and content which Jesus put into the phrase 'Our Father'
when it is addressed to God.

It is often easiest to see the sheer newness of some discovery
of the mind of man, not in the first instance by looking at it, but
by looking at the beliefs of men before the discovery was made,
and at the beliefs of men, who after it was made disregarded it or
refused to accept it. We will, therefore, best see the sheer newness
of Jesus' idea of God by looking at men's ideas of God before he
came into the world.

The two great pre-Christian philosophies by which men lived
in the Graeco-Roman world were Stoicism and Epicureanism.
For the Stoic the one essential attribute of God was *apatheia*.
*Apatheia* in Greek is not apathy in the ordinary English sense of

the term. In English apathy is the indifference of one who need not and should not feel indifferent. *Apatheia* in Greek is the essential inability to experience any feeling at all. The Greek argument was simple and logical. If a person can experience the feeling of joy or grief, or love or hate, it means that some other person can affect him. Some other person by his attitude can bring to him gladness or grief, can affect and change the feelings of his heart. Now to be able to affect another person is at least for the moment to have some kind of power over him. But clearly, as the Greeks saw it, no one can have any power over God. And the only way to ensure that this is so is to assume as a first principle that God, just because he is God, is entirely incapable of any feeling. He is *apathes*, passionless, emotionless, essentially indifferent.

For the Epicureans the supreme quality in life was *ataraxia*, by which they meant complete calm, perfect serenity. The Epicureans went on to argue that if God were involved in the affairs of the world, then his serenity would be gone for ever. So for him the essence of Godhead is complete and total detachment from the world. The gods may see the world, but they are completely detached from it. It is in fact precisely that serene unmoved detachment which makes them gods. Tennyson in the *Choric Song* in *The Lotos-Eaters* perfectly caught the Epicurean conception of the gods:

> For they lie beside their nectar, and the bolts are hurl'd
> Far below them in the valleys, and the clouds are lightly curl'd
> Round their golden houses, girdled with the gleaming world;
> Where they smile in secret, looking over wasted lands,
> Blight and famine, plague and earthquake, roaring deeps and fiery
> sands,
> Clanging fights, and flaming towns, and sinking ships and praying
> hands.

Here is the perfect picture of the Epicurean gods, insulated from all emotion and detached from all action and isolated from all interest.

Now let us take three pictures from the Old Testament. When we take these three pictures from the Old Testament, let us be quite clear what we are doing. We are not belittling the Old Testament; we are simply saying that the Old Testament thinkers did not know God as Jesus knew him. After all, if the Old Testament thinkers already perfectly knew God, there would have been no necessity for Jesus to come. It was because men did not, and could not by themselves, know what God was like that God did come to men in Jesus Christ.

First, let us take the great picture from Job 38 and 39. These two chapters are supreme not only in the dramatic poetry of the Old Testament but in the dramatic poetry of the world. The Lord answers the tortured and agonized Job out of the whirlwind. 'Where were you when I laid the foundations of the earth? Have you commanded the morning since your days began? Have you entered into the springs of the sea? Have you comprehended the expanse of the earth? Have you entered the storehouses of the snow? Can you bind the chains of the Pleiades, or loose the cords of Orion? Do you give the horse his might? Do you clothe his neck with strength?' (Job 38.4, 12, 16, 18, 22, 31; 39.19). These chapters are the most awe-inspiring divine bombardment of Job, and the whole grim and terrible point of them is that God is saying to Job: 'What right have you to speak to me, or to question me?' It would be difficult to imagine Jesus speaking to any physically tortured and heart-broken man like that.

Second, let us take Jeremiah's parable of the potter (Jeremiah 18.1–11). Jeremiah saw the potter at work. In the making of a vessel the vessel was marred, and the potter simply wiped it out and began over again. 'Behold,' Jeremiah takes God to say, 'like the clay in the potter's hand, so are you in my hand, O house of

Israel. Can I not do with you as the potter has done?' (Jeremiah 18.6). Here is the picture of a God who will do with living man what the potter does with soulless clay. On this view man has no more rights in the eyes of God than a lump of misshapen clay has in the eyes of the potter. It is surely impossible to imagine Jesus speaking of men as if they were *things*.

Third, let us take the picture of the Psalmist. In Psalm 24.3–5 the Psalmist lays down the conditions of approach to God as he sees them:

> Who shall ascend the hill of the Lord?
> > And who shall stand in his holy place?
> He who has clean hands and a pure heart,
> > who does not lift up his soul to what is false,
> > and does not swear deceitfully.
> He will receive blessing from the Lord,
> > and vindication from the God of his salvation.

To anyone who thinks of the meaning of these words, apart from their poetry, they are terrible words, for, as he hears them, he hears the door to God slam in his face, for very certainly no human being can fulfil these conditions. It is impossible to conceive of the Jesus who said: 'I came not to call the righteous, but sinners,' speaking like that (Matthew 9.13).

Here are three Old Testament pictures of God which can only leave us terrified and afraid, and yet that is the way in which men thought of God before Jesus Christ.

Let us add to this three modern examples. James Stewart quotes two lines from a poem of Thomas Hardy and a saying of Voltaire. Thomas Hardy asks what can possibly be the use of prayer when we have no one to whom to pray except,

> The dreaming, dark, dumb Thing
> That turns the handle of the idle Show.

Voltaire's final verdict on life was, 'A bad joke.' 'Ring down the curtain, the farce is done.' H. G. Wells in one of his novels painted the picture of a man defeated by the stress and strain and tension of modern life. His doctor wisely told him that his only hope of retaining his sanity was to find fellowship with God. 'What?' said the man. 'That up there – having fellowship with me? I would as soon think of cooling my throat with the milky way or shaking hands with the stars.'

Here then are the verdicts of those who do not know God in Jesus Christ. The Stoic sees his emotionless God; the Epicurean sees his utterly detached gods; the Old Testament writers paint in the most splendid but terrible terms the might and majesty and power and holiness of God; the modern writers can see nothing in God to which the man with the broken heart can appeal. And now let us turn to see something of that which Jesus put into this word father.

To begin with, we must look at the word *Father* itself. Great as it is, at first sight, to apply this word to God, it is still greater when we penetrate further into its meaning. In Gethsemane Jesus prayed, 'Abba, Father' (Mark 14.36); and Paul twice writes to his people that we through the Holy Spirit can pray in the same way, and that we can use the same word as Jesus did when we too pray to God (Romans 8.15; Galatians 4.6). This word *abba* is more than *father*. It was the word by which a little child in Palestine addressed his father in the home circle as *jaba* still is in Arabic today. There is only one possible English translation of this word in any ordinary use of it, and that is 'Daddy'. Of course, to translate it that way in the New Testament would sound bizarre and grotesque, but it does at once give us the atmosphere in which we come to God; we come to God with the simple trust and confidence with which a little child comes to a father whom he knows and loves and trusts. And Jeremias points out that there is no parallel in the whole of Jewish literature for the application of this word to God.

We would hardly need to go any further. Could there be any greater contrast to the Stoic *apatheia*, to the Epicurean detachment, to the Old Testament distance, to the modern doubt of the love of God, than this word *abba*? The plain fact is that no one in all the world had ever thought of God like that before, and to this day, apart from Jesus Christ, no one can think of God like this. The minute we use this word two things are settled straight away.

It settles once and for all *our relationship to God*. This is the spirit, this is the confidence, this is the intimacy with which we come to God.

When we go to Jesus' own words, we can still further fill out the meaning of this word.

(i) First and foremost, it tells us that *God cares*. So far from being isolated, detached, insulated against all emotion, God cares for men with the constant love of a father, and with such a passion of love that in the end in Jesus Christ he suffered the agony of the Cross. The word has in it all the passion of the love of God.

(ii) Furthermore, we learn that this love of God is *a quite undeserved love*. Jesus cites it as typical of this fatherly love of God that God makes his sun to rise on the evil and the good and sends his rain on the just and the unjust (Matthew 5.45). This love of God is not kept for the good son and the son who never disobeys; it even reaches out to the son who goes his own way and breaks his father's heart and comes wretchedly home because he has nowhere else to go (Luke 15.11–32). There is no question of needing clean hands and a pure heart before we can enter into that love. God the Father loves us with a love which will never let us go.

(iii) And yet in spite of that *this love of God has its own rewards*. God in his own way, all unseen and all unknown, rewards the son who does his Father's will (Matthew 6.4, 6, 18). God has two kinds of sons, the sons who break his heart and the sons who delight his heart, and there are precious things for those who do their Father's will. The disobedient son is not shut out, but there are things for the obedient son that the disobedient son can never know, until he turns and submits to his Father's love.

(iv) This fatherly love of God is a *practical love*. It knows well that we need food and clothing and all the necessary things of life. Our Father knows that we need these things (Matthew 6.8, 32; Luke 12.30). When we go to God in prayer, our prayers need not be entirely 'spiritual' and 'religious'. We can pray to God for our practical, worrying, every-day needs. There is nothing which we cannot take to God in prayer.

(v) So great is this love that it covers *the whole creation of God*. God loves even the animals and the birds and the flowers, every living thing his hands have made. And the wonderful thing about this fatherhood of God is that it is not only universal, as wide as the world, it is *unbelievably detailed*. The same saying of Jesus is reported differently in Matthew and in Luke. In Matthew 10.29 it runs:

> Are not two sparrows sold for a penny? And not one of them will fall to the ground without your Father's will.

In Luke 12.6 it runs:

> Are not five sparrows sold for two pennies? And not one of them is forgotten before God.

In Palestine a purchaser could buy two sparrows for one penny; but if he was prepared to spend two pennies he got, not four, but *five* sparrows. The extra sparrow was thrown into the bargain; it was quite worthless; it had no value at all; it mattered to no one; *but even that extra sparrow matters to God*. Surely never did Jesus say so clearly that there is no one who does not matter in the sight of God.

Paul Tournier, the great Christian doctor, tells a tragic thing. In *A Doctor's Casebook* he writes: 'There was one patient of mine, the youngest daughter in a large family, which the father found it difficult to support. One day she heard him mutter despairingly, referring to herself: "We could well have done without that one!"' That is precisely what God can never say. In the same book Paul Tournier notes another thing. God says to Moses: 'I know thee *by name*' (Exodus 33.17). He says to Cyrus: 'I am the Lord, which call thee *by thy name*' (Isaiah 45.3). One of the features of the Bible is whole chapters of names, of genealogies. There was a time when Paul Tournier thought that these chapters could well have been omitted from the Bible, and then he came to see that they are the symbol of the infinite number of people whom God knows *by name*. The love of God is so detailed that the worthless sparrow matters to him, that there is no one whom he does not know by name. In point of fact the saying about the sparrow may be even more wonderful yet. 'Not one of them will fall to the ground without your Father's will.' We might think that that refers to the *death* of a sparrow. But my old teacher J. E. McFadyen used to love to suggest that, if we put that saying back into Aramaic, it may well mean, not that God sees it, if a sparrow *falls* to the ground, but if a sparrow *lights* on the ground. Every time the sparrow hops on the ground God sees it and knows.

Every time we pray, 'Our Father,' we can know for certain that for God no one is lost in the crowd; that if we matter to no one else, we matter to God; that if no one else cares for us, God cares. Here is something to lift up our hearts every time we pray our Lord's prayer.

We began by saying that two things are settled by this address to God. It settles our relationship to God; but equally it settles *our relationship to our fellow men*. The word before Father is *our*. The very use of that word ends all exclusiveness. If God is *our* Father, then our fellow man is our brother. The only possible basis for democracy is the conviction of the fatherhood of God. The only value that man possesses as man is that he is the child of God. Nationalism, racialism, snobbery, class distinction, the colour bar, *apartheid* stand uncompromisingly condemned in the two words which open our Lord's prayer. If we pray those words and hate or despise our brother man, then the prayer is a mockery and we make ourselves liars.

Our Father – we might almost say that a man need go no further than these two words in his prayers, for here once and for all there are settled our relationship to God and our relationship to our fellow men. Here are the two words which invite us to come into God's presence with childlike confidence and boldness and which forbid us to do anything but love any man.

# CHAPTER THREE

# Hallowed be Thy Name

It may well be that of all the petitions of the Lord's Prayer this prayer that God's name should be hallowed is the petition to which most people would find it most difficult to attach any definite and precise meaning, if they were asked what they meant when they were praying it. I once knew a small boy who always prayed it in a form all his own: 'Herald be thy name'! And no doubt he was thinking of the 'herald angels' of the Christmas hymn. Since this is so, we must begin with the basic task of establishing the meaning of the word in this petition.

Let us begin by tracing the various translations of this petition which different translators have offered. These translations fall into four groups.

(i) There are the translations which use the word *hallowed*. This is the oldest translation of all. It goes back to Alfred the Great: '*Sic gehalyed dhin noma*'; and to Wicliffe: 'Halewed be thy name'. This word hallowed then came down to us via Tyndale, Coverdale, the Great Bible, the Geneva Bible, the Authorized Version, and the Revised Version. It is in the modern versions of Ronald A. Knox and of E. V. Rieu; and it is the word which is used in the New English Bible. From the first of the translations to the last this word *hallowed* is used. It has a long and honourable lineage, and even the most modern translators have felt that there was nothing better.

(ii) There are the translations which use the word *holy*. Typical of them is Weymouth: 'May thy name be kept holy.' And in one form or another this is the translation of C. Kingsley Williams and of the Twentieth Century New Testament. It is the alternative translation of the Amplified New Testament: 'Hallowed (kept holy) be your name.' As we shall see, this translation is indeed very close to the original.

(iii) There are the translations which use the word *sanctified*. Typical of this translation is the Douai-Rheims version: 'sanctified be thy name.' This is also the word used by Schonfield in the Authentic New Testament. This translation is not really different, for in fact all that it does is to use the latinized form of the word *to hallow*.

(iv) There are the translations which go, as we might say, a little further afield to find a rendering. Moffatt and Goodspeed uses the word *revered*: 'Thy (your) name be revered.' Kenneth Wuest uses the word *venerated*: 'Let your name be venerated.' J. B. Phillips uses the word *honoured*: 'May your name be honoured.'

We may finally look at a translation which is not so much a translation as a curiosity. One of the most extraordinary of all modern translations is that of Edward Harwood, published in 1768 under the long title, *A Liberal translation of the New Testament: being an Attempt to translate the Sacred Writings with the same Freedom, Spirit and Elegance, with which other English Translations from the Greek Classics have lately been executed.* Harwood, whose translation F. F. Bruce not unfairly calls 'a literary curio', was perhaps the first of the paraphrasers, and his translation of the opening clauses of the Lord's Prayer, 'Our Father which art in Heaven: Hallowed be thy name', runs:

> O Thou great governour and parent of universal nature – who manifestest thy glory to the blessed inhabitants of heaven – may all thy rational creatures in all the parts of thy boundless dominion be happy in the knowledge of thy existence and providence, and celebrate thy perfections in a manner most worthy thy nature and perfective of their own.

What Harwood is trying to do is clear enough, but whether or not he succeeded in doing it is quite another question!

Let us, then, turn to the definition of the meaning of the words in this petition and let us start with the meaning of the word *name*.

In biblical times the *name* stood for much more than the name by which a person is called in the modern sense of the term. The name stood for the whole character of the person as it was known, manifested, or revealed. As Origen puts it in commenting on this petition of the Lord's Prayer (*On Prayer* 24.2, 3) name is a term which summarizes and manifests the personal character of him who is named. The name stands for 'the personal and incommunicable character' of the person. The *name* of God, therefore, stands for the nature and the character and the personality of God as they have been revealed to men. This becomes quite clear when we see the way in which the *name* is used in Scripture. The Psalmist (Psalm 9.10) says:

> Those who know thy name put their trust in thee.

That clearly does not mean that those who know God's name in the English sense of the term will willingly trust him; it means that those who know the character and nature and personality of God, those who know what God is like as he has revealed himself to be, will willingly trust in him. Again, the Psalmist (Psalm 20.7) says:

> Some boast of chariots, and some of horses;
> but we boast of the name of the Lord our God.

That is to say, some regard chariots and horses as their most powerful possessions, but to us the greatest thing of all is the nature of God as he has revealed himself to us. In John (17.6) Jesus says:

I have manifested thy name to the men whom thou gavest me out
of the world.

In effect, that means that Jesus clearly told his own men *what God
is like*, what the nature and the character and the personality of
God truly are. The name can stand for nothing less than God
himself. The Old Testament can talk of 'blaspheming the Name'
– the RSV prints *Name* with a capital letter – and that clearly
means insulting God himself. (Leviticus 24.16).

We begin, then, with the fact that the name means the nature,
the character, the personality of God as they have been revealed
to us.

We now move on to examine the meaning of the word *hallow*.
In Greek the word is *hagiazein*, which is clearly connected with the
word *hagios*, which is generally translated *holy*. *Hagiazein* is practically non-existent in secular Greek, but in biblical Greek there is
ample material to define its meaning. It has two basic meanings.
First, it means to make an ordinary secular thing holy, by certain
rituals or by bringing it into contact with things which are holy.
That is obviously not the meaning here. Nothing that man can do
can make the name of God holy in that sense, for that would
imply that to start with the name of God is *not* holy. But, second,
*hagiazein* means to treat as holy, that is, *to hold sacred*. To hallow a
thing is to regard and to treat that thing as holy and sacred. But
what does that mean? We can best come at this from remembering the meaning of *hagios*. *Hagios* is the adjective meaning *holy*;
but the basic idea behind it is the idea of *difference*. That which is
*hagios* is different from ordinary things; it belongs to a different
sphere of quality and of being. That is why God is supremely The
Holy One, for God supremely belongs to a different sphere of
life and being.

This meaning becomes even clearer when we examine the
word in use. The commandment is to remember the Sabbath day

to keep it *holy* (Exodus 20.8). That is to say, the Sabbath day is to be regarded and to be kept as different from other days. The instruction is *to consecrate* the priest (Leviticus 21.8). This also is the word *hagiazein*, and clearly the meaning is to set the priest apart so that he is different from other and from ordinary men, so that, we might now say, he is different from *lay men*.

When we arrive at this stage, we can see that the meaning of the word *hagiazein* is beginning to acquire the meaning of *reverence*, for reverence is the characteristic attitude to that which is different, that which belongs to a sphere of being other than our own. There is an Old Testament passage (Numbers 20.1–11; cp. Deuteronomy 32.51) which well illustrates the meaning of this word. The story is that the children of Israel in their journeyings in the wilderness were near to perishing of thirst, and were full of bitter complaints. God instructed Moses to take his rod and to speak to the rock and to tell the rock to give forth water. But Moses, instead of only speaking to the rock, in his anger and irritation struck the rock. Then there comes the statement:

> Because you did not believe in me to *sanctify* me in the eyes of the people of Israel you shall not bring this assembly into the land which I have given them.

The verb to sanctify is *hagiazein*; Moffatt translates it, 'because you did not vindicate my honour', and the Smith-Goodspeed translation is, 'because you did not pay me my due honour'. Basically, the idea is that the action of Moses was an action of *irreverence* in that it implied disobedience to God and distrust of God; by, as it were, taking the law into his own hands, Moses had been guilty of irreverence towards God.

So, then, we arrive at the conclusion that *to hallow* means *to reverence*. We have now defined the meaning of the two terms in this petition. The *name* of God is the character, nature and personality of God, as he has revealed them to us, in the Scriptures, in the world which he has made, and especially in Jesus Christ our Lord. *To hallow* is *to hold in reverence*. If we, then, pray, 'Hallowed be thy name', the prayer means, 'May you be given that unique reverence which your character and nature and personality, as you have revealed them to us, demand.' The prayer is that God may be given that reverence which his divine being demands and necessitates, and which, through his self-revelation, we well know to be due to him. We get exactly the same idea in regard to Jesus in 1 Peter (3.15) where Peter bids his people: 'Reverence (*hagiazein*) Christ as Lord.' To Jesus there must be given the reverence which his lordship demands.

This conclusion is underlined by the fact that sometimes the Greek fathers use certain other words as the equivalent of *hagiazein*. Chrysostom equates it with *doxazein*, which means *to glorify* or *to honour*. Origen equates it with *hupsoun*, which means *to exalt* or *to lift on high*. And later *hagiazein* is often expressed by the word *eulogein*, which means *to bless* or *to praise*. To hallow God's name is to give God the reverence, the honour, the glory, the praise, the exaltation which his character demands. Calvin puts it this way: 'That God's name should be hallowed is nothing other than to say that God should have his own honour, of which he is worthy, so that men should never think or speak of him without the greatest veneration.'

We have no sooner arrived at this conclusion than we see at once that one possible threat and danger is removed. When we set down the relationship between God and man that is involved in the word Father, and especially in the word *Abba*, there must be in our minds the awareness that it is possible for a certain sentimentality to creep in. No doctrine is more liable to be sentimentalized than the doctrine of the fatherhood of God. But one thing becomes clear to anyone who knows anything about Jewish religion and worship – the fact that any such sentimentalization is for a Jew essentially impossible. For a Jew God is supremely

The Wholly Other; no Jew ever could think of God without reverence.

One of the most interesting facts about Judaism is that when a Jew called God Father he almost always added to the word Father some other words which conserved the majesty and the glory of God. So in Ecclesiasticus the prayer of the preacher is (Sir. 23.1)

> O Lord, Father and Ruler of my life

and again (Sir. 23.4):

> O Lord, Father and God of my life.

In 3 Maccabees (6.2–4) before the writer prays to God, 'O Father', he has already prayed immediately before:

> King of great power, most high, almighty God, who governest all
> creation with loving-kindness.

In the greatest of all the Synagogue prayers, the prayer known variously as the *Shermoneh 'Esreh*, that is, the Eighteen Benedictions, or the *Amidah* prayer, or the *Tefillah*, which means, as it were, the prayer *par excellence*, the fifth and sixth Benedictions run:

> Cause us to return, O our Father, to thy law, and draw us near, O
> King, to thy service, and restore us in perfect penitence to thy pres-
> ence. Blessed art thou, O Lord, who delightest in repentance.
>
> Forgive us, our Father, for we have sinned; pardon us, our
> King, for we have transgressed; ready to pardon and forgive thou
> art. Blessed art thou, O Lord, most gracious, who dost abundantly
> pardon.

Nothing is more characteristic of Jewish prayer than the combination of the titles Father and King and Lord in addresses to God.

In the *Ahabah rabbah* prayer which comes second after the Shema (Jewish prayers are often known by their opening words, and these words mean *with abounding love*) there comes the petition:

> Our Father, our King, for our fathers' sake who trusted in thee, and whom thou didst teach the statutes of life, be thou gracious to us likewise and teach us.

In the famous *Kaddish* prayer which introduces the various parts of the Synagogue service there is an almost exact parallel to the first two clauses of the Lord's Prayer:

> Magnified and sanctified be his great name in the world which he hath created according to his will. May he establish his kingdom during your life and during your days, and during the life of all the house of Israel even speedily and at a near time, and say ye Amen.

On the ten penitential days at the time of the Day of Atonement the Jews pray the great *Abinu Malkenu* (Our Father, our King) prayer. It has forty-four petitions all beginning, 'Our Father, our King', of which some are:

> Our Father, our King, we have sinned before thee.
> Our Father, our King, we have none other King but thee.
> Our Father, our King, bring us back before thee in perfect repentance.
> Our Father, our King, vouchsafe to write us in the Book of Redemption.
> Our Father, our King, hear us, though no good works of our own be in us.
> We will sanctify also thy name throughout the world, O God, the God of our fathers, reign thou over the whole world in thy glory

There may be a modern danger of sentimentalizing the idea of God as Father; it is not a danger into which any Jew would ever have fallen. The Jews called God Father, and loved to call him so, but they never forgot that he was also the King and Lord of all the earth. Reverence was never in any danger of being obliterated by sentimentality.

So here in the Lord's Prayer we pray not only to our Father, but to our *Father who is in heaven*, and then we pray that God may receive the reverence which his unique character and nature deserve and demand. We have now to go on to see what in actual practice in life it means to hallow the name of God, what it means to give God that unique place which his nature and character and personality demand. In other words, we have to try to find out *what true reverence is*.

There is one basic prerequisite without which reverence cannot even begin to exist. That prerequisite was perfectly stated by the writer to the Hebrews (11.6): 'Whoever would draw near to God must believe that he exists and that he rewards those who seek him.' That is to say, there can be no such thing as reverence without the twin basic beliefs, first, that God exists, and, second, that God is interested in the attitude and actions of men towards himself. The Bible itself never seeks to prove the existence of God. In geometry there are certain truths which are called axioms. Axioms are not themselves proved; they are the basic truths which are the foundation of all reasoning and of all proofs. For the biblical writers God is an axiom, more, God is *the* axiom, the fact of whose existence is the basic fact of life. The biblical writers would have said that they no more needed to prove the existence of God than they needed to prove the existence of their wife or of their closest friend. They did not need to prove the existence of God, because they daily met God; they did not need to argue about God, because they daily and hourly met God. As for the fact that God is interested in man's response and reaction to himself, to the Christian thinker there is no need to go beyond the incarnation to find proof of that. The interest of God in men is such that he in Jesus Christ entered into life to bring men to himself. The Christian can never have any doubt that God 'exists and that he rewards those who seek him.'

How, then, shall we express this reverence for the God who exists and the God who is interested in us? Tholuck finds that the commentators on this petition interpret its obligation in three different ways.

(i) They interpret it, as we might say, from the negative angle, and take it to mean that God's name should never be profaned but always named with reverence. This is obviously a narrow interpretation, and has to do with a man's speaking and nothing else.

(ii) They interpret it more positively to mean that God must be praised and glorified in words. This would mean that we hallow the name of God and that we reverence him in the prayers and praises of the liturgy and in the acts of worship in the narrower sense of the term. This is still a narrow interpretation, and confines this necessary reverence to the worship men offer within the Church.

(iii) They interpret it to mean that God must be reverenced in the heart, and that our outward walk and conversation should continually show this inward reverence, since from such a life others too are moved to reverence God. This in effect means that we must reverence God and hallow the name of God in the actions of everyday life.

There is no doubt which is the correct interpretation. The reverence which is demanded cannot be confined to words; it cannot be confined to the liturgy and praises of the Church, however splendid they may be; it must be lived and demonstrated in every moment of our lives, both in the Church and in the world. We find in the early fathers specially illuminating interpretations of this petition, and always along these lines. They see this reverence exemplified in three directions.

(i) We reverence God *when our beliefs concerning God are such as*

*are worthy of God.* That is to say true doctrine and true teaching are
reverence for God; false doctrine and false teaching are irreverence to God. Origen (*On Prayer* 24) brings this out. God has
revealed himself as HE WHO IS (Exodus 3.14). Now everyone
makes his own suppositions about God; everyone knows something about God; but man being man can only grasp a very little
of the holiness of God. And, because we are so liable to make
mistakes, and to confuse partial truths with the whole truth, we
are taught to pray 'that our concept of God may be hallowed
amongst us'. 'The man who brings into his concept of God ideas
which have no place there takes the name of the Lord God in
vain.' Since the *name* of God means *the nature and the character* of
God, anyone who brings into his idea of God thoughts and con-
ceptions which are alien to the true character of God is guilty of
irreverence and of failure to hallow the name of God.

To take the obvious example, the Greeks with their stories of
the wars and battles and struggles and quarrels, the loves and
hates and seductions and adulteries of the gods, were in fact
guilty of irreverence, for they were bringing into the conception
of God things which had no right to be there. But Christians
themselves have been far from guiltless in this matter. Very often
men have been repelled by ideas of God which show God as
savage, vindictive, harsh and cruel, and the very opposite of the
God whom we see in Jesus Christ. There will be those who will
not agree, but it may well be that those who presented men with
the conception of a God who banned unbaptized children from
heaven and who predestined one man to heaven and another to
hell for his own glory have been guilty of the sin of irreverence.
There have been times when God has been presented as a God
of battles and a kind of nationalistic ally. There have been times
when men have drawn a picture of God to suit their own theories
of racial superiority. There have been times when men used their
own ideas of God to erect a barrier to all social progress, and

when they did indeed make religion the opiate of the people, when they made religion an argument for maintaining the *status quo*. There have been theories of the Atonement which at least by implication set over against each other a God of avenging justice and a Christ of sacrificial love. John Wesley was right when he said of one who had such beliefs: 'Your God is my devil.'

To allow into our conception of God things which are unworthy of God, and things which can have no place in the God who is the God and Father of our Lord Jesus Christ is to fail to hallow the name of God; it is to be guilty of irreverence, and, worst of all, it has been the reason why countless thousands of men and women have been repelled by the Church and its teaching. If we are to hallow God's name, we must see to it that our conception of God is truly Christian.

(ii) We reverence God and we hallow God's name, *when our life is such that it brings honour to God and attracts others to him*. This is an idea to which the early fathers return again and again. Cyril of Jerusalem (*Catechetical Lecture* 23) begins by saying that quite clearly God's name is in itself and in its nature holy, no matter what we may say or do, or not say or not do. The prayer cannot possibly mean that God's name should become holy from not being holy. We are to pray this prayer because God's name 'becomes holy in us, when we are made holy, and do things worthy of holiness.' Cyprian (*On the Lord's Prayer* 12) says that it is obviously impossible that we should wish for God that he should be hallowed by our prayer; what we do ask is that 'his name should be hallowed in us'. Tertullian (*On Prayer* 3) says exactly the same thing. The prayer is that 'God's name may be hallowed in us'. Augustine (*The Sermon on the Mount* 5.19) makes exactly the same point. It is not that God's name is not already holy. What we do pray for is that men should regard it as holy, that is to say, that God may become so near and dear to us that we will esteem nothing more holy than his name and dread nothing more than to offend it.

This is worked out most fully and most relevantly by Gregory of Nyssa in his third Sermon on the Lord's Prayer. We pray this prayer because in itself human nature is too weak to achieve any of the things which it well knows it ought to achieve. The good can only be accomplished in us by divine aid. And of all good things the most important for us is *that God should be glorified through our lives*. This, says Gregory, will become quite clear, if we look at it from the negative angle first. Paul condemns those (Romans 2.24) through whom God has to say: 'The name of God is blasphemed among the Gentiles.' The Christian is living in a pagan environment; and, if the heathen see the Christian living an immoral, an irreligious and an unlovely life, they attribute the ugliness of that life not to the fault of the individual Christian, but to the Christianity of which the individual Christian is the sample and representative. Not the Christian but Christianity is blamed for such conduct. The prayer really means: 'Let the name of God be hallowed in me, so that men may see our good works and glorify our Father who is in heaven.' Any reasonable man will in honesty be compelled to glorify God 'if he sees in those who believe in him a life firmly established in virtue … purged from all sin, above any suspicion of evil, and shining with temperance and holy prudence.'

Then Gregory goes on to describe the kind of life which the man who in his life hallows the name of God will live:

> A man who leads such a life will oppose fortitude to the assaults of the passions; since he partakes of the requirements of life only as far as is necessary, he is in no way softened by the luxuries of the body and is an utter stranger to revelry and laziness as well as to boastful conceit. He touches the earth but lightly with the tip of his toes, for he is not engulfed by the pleasurable enjoyments of its life, but is above all deceit that comes by the senses. And so, even although in the flesh, he strives after the immaterial life. He counts

the possession of virtues the only riches, familiarity with God the only nobility. His only privilege and power is the mastery of self so as not to be a slave to human passions. He is saddened if his life in this material world be prolonged; like those who are seasick he hastens to reach the port of rest.

He goes on to say that, when he prays this petition, what he is really praying is:

May I become through thy help blameless, just and pious, may I abstain from every evil, speak the truth, and do justice. May I walk in the straight path, shining with temperance, adorned with incorruption, beautiful through wisdom and prudence. May I meditate upon the things that are above and despise what is earthly, showing the angelic way of life.... For a man can glorify God in no other way save by his virtue which bears witness that the Divine Power is the cause of his goodness.

Here in truth this petition is driven home to us. The name of God can only be hallowed when every action of our life is a witness to our faith in him, and when we continuously bring credit to the name we bear. The early fathers stress this with such intensity because they were living in a pagan environment, and the only way in which Christianity could spread and could conquer the world was by the individual Christian living a life of such beauty and goodness and truth that others might wish to share the secret of that loveliness. The one thing which was fatal was a life which brought the Christian faith and the Christian Church into disrepute. The plain fact is that the situation has not changed. It may be that we do not now live in a society which is hostile to Christianity; we live in a society in which Christianity and the Church have become irrelevant. And, if the Christian is just as likely to collapse under sorrow, if his life is just as frustrated and unsatisfied as the life of the non-Christian, if he is just as worried and anxious, just as nervous and restless, just as guilty of petty dishonesty, of self-seeking, of measuring everything by material values as the man who makes no profession of Christianity, then quite clearly no one will want Christianity because the obvious conclusion is that it makes no difference anyway. Nietschze, the famous German pagan philosopher, said a thing which flings the challenge at every professing Christian: 'Show me that you are redeemed and then I will believe in your redeemer.' The very essence of this petition is that in it we pray that God may enable us to show that we are redeemed, so that in our lives he may be glorified, and so that through us others may come to desire the secret which we possess. This petition prays that we may be enabled so to show Christ to men that men may desire Christ.

(iii) It is quite clear that this petition represents not only a prayer on our part, but also a demand on the part of God, a demand which without God's help we cannot fulfil. If, then, we are to hallow the name of God, we must first of all enthrone God within our hearts. In his commentary on this petition Origen (*On Prayer* 24.4) has a lovely, if maybe far-fetched, piece of exegesis. He identifies *hallowing* the name of God with *extolling* the name of God. He then quotes Psalm 30.1 : 'I will extol thee, O Lord, for thou hast drawn me up, and hast not let my foes rejoice over me.' In this Psalm the Psalmist *extols*, *hallows*, the name of God. Then Origen goes on to quote the title at the head of this Psalm: 'A Psalm of David. A Song at the Dedication of the Temple.' Then he draws his deduction: 'We extol God when we dedicate within ourselves a house to God.' To extol God, to hallow God's name, must in the last analysis mean that we make our hearts his temple and his dwelling-place, for only when he dwells within our hearts will our lives truly honour him and truly draw others to him.

Hallowed be thy name – here is the petition which saves the idea of the Fatherhood of God from all sentimentality and which sets down in unmistakable terms the inescapable obligation of reverence. In it we pray that God himself should enable us to give to him the unique place which his nature and character and personality as revealed in Jesus Christ demand and deserve. And we give him that place only when our conception of him is truly Christian and has no dregs of unlovely unworthiness in it, and when our lives are so clothed with the beauty of holiness that they are a continual invitation to share the secret which we possess in Jesus Christ. And we know that we can never do that until we enthrone him as King within our hearts.

In his Larger Catechism Martin Luther asks the question: 'How is it (God's name) hallowed amongst us?' And he gives the answer: 'When our life and doctrine are truly Christian.' So, then, this petition is at one and the same time a challenge to Christian action and an invitation to Christian commitment.

# CHAPTER FOUR

# Thy Kingdom Come

It would be both possible and natural to hold that 'Thy Kingdom come' is the central petition of the Lord's Prayer, for it is quite certain that the Kingdom of God was the central message and proclamation of Jesus. When Mark tells how Jesus first publicly emerged upon the scene, he summarizes the message of Jesus: 'The time is fulfilled, and the Kingdom of God is at hand; repent, and believe in the gospel' (Mark 1.14; cp. Matthew 4.17). Luke tells how Jesus told his disciples that they must be moving on. 'I must preach the good news of the Kingdom of God to the other cities also, for I was sent for this purpose' (Luke 4.43). The announcement of the Kingdom was nothing less than the purpose for which Jesus came into the world. The centrality of the idea of the Kingdom is made clear from the fact that the phrase the Kingdom of God, or the Kingdom of Heaven, appears 49 times in Matthew, 16 times in Mark and 38 times in Luke.

It is quite clear that, if this idea is so central to the message of Jesus, we must clearly understand what the Kingdom is, and what its relevance is to us, before we can genuinely pray this prayer. There are two quite general facts that we must first note.

(i) It might be better to talk of the *kingship* or of the *reign* of God. In modem speech the word kingdom is apt to mean a certain territory or area of land, as, for instance, when we speak of the kingdom of Belgium or the kingdom of Holland, or the kingdom of Great Britain and Ireland. But in the New Testament the kingdom is not a territory; it is the reign of God. 'The Kingdom of God is at hand' means 'God is on the point of beginning his reign; the kingship, the royal power, of God within the world, is about to begin.'

(ii) The New Testament uses two phrases, the Kingdom of God and the Kingdom of Heaven. The two phrases mean exactly the same and it is an error to try to make any distinction between them. The facts are that Matthew hardly ever speaks of the Kingdom of God and practically always speaks of the Kingdom of Heaven, while Mark and Luke practically never speak of the Kingdom of Heaven and always speak of the Kingdom of God. The reason for that variation in practice is this. A devout Jew was very hesitant to take the name of God upon his lips at all. If it was possible he would always use some reverential periphrasis. The obvious periphrasis for God is heaven. Matthew is the most Jewish of the Gospel writers, and to avoid using the name of God he speaks rather of the Kingdom of Heaven, while Mark and Luke, being much less influenced by Jewish background, do not hesitate to speak of the Kingdom of God.

One of the most curious facts of the Gospels is that there is no definition of the Kingdom. The Kingdom is described in pictures and in analogies and in its demands and effects, but it is never in so many words defined. If we are to discuss it, we must have a working definition of it. Hebrew literary style is marked by the continuous use of parallelism. It is the common Hebrew practice to say everything twice; and the second arm of the parallel restates, or amplifies, or explains the first. This Hebrew characteristic is exemplified best of all in almost every verse of the Psalms.

> The Lord of hosts is with us;
> The God of Jacob is our refuge.

> (Psalm 46.7)

> The Lord is thy keeper;
> The Lord is thy shade on thy right hand.

> (Psalm 121.5)

In the Lord's Prayer two petitions appear side by side:

> Thy Kingdom come;
> Thy will be done in earth as it is in heaven.

> (Matthew 6.10)

If we may assume that here there is an instance of normal Hebrew parallelism, and that the second arm of the parallel explains and defines the first, then we can arrive at the definition: The Kingdom of God is a society upon earth in which God's will is as perfectly done as it is in heaven. That is to say, to do the will of God and to be in the Kingdom are one and the same thing. To be a citizen of any kingdom, and to be a subject of any king, necessarily involve obedience to the laws of that kingdom and to the commands of that king. To be a member of the Kingdom of God necessarily involves acceptance of the will of God.

This at once explains Jesus' place in the Kingdom, and it also explains certain puzzling New Testament sayings. In Matthew 11.11 Jesus is reported as saying: 'Truly I say to you, among those born of women there has arisen no one greater than John the Baptist; yet he who is least in the Kingdom of Heaven is greater than he' (cp. Luke 7.28). The implication is that with the coming of Jesus and the coming of the Kingdom something completely new entered into life. What is that new thing? Let us remember our definition of the Kingdom; to be in the Kingdom means the perfect acceptance and the perfect performance of the will of God. Jesus Christ was the one and only person who ever fully accepted and fully carried out the will of God. *Therefore with Jesus the Kingdom came*. In him the Kingdom arrived. He incarnates and embodies the Kingdom. Jesus not only *proclaimed* the Kingdom;

he *is* the Kingdom demonstrated in human life. He brought to men the message and the manifestation of the Kingdom.

Immediately we see the Kingdom in terms of the will of God, the Kingdom becomes a personal thing. The Kingdom of God is not something which in the first place involves nations and peoples and countries. The Kingdom of God is something which begins with me. To speak of the Kingdom is not to state a theological doctrine; it is not to institute a political programme; it is to confront oneself with a personal challenge in which we either accept or refuse the will of God for us. The Chinese Christian wisely prayed: 'Lord, revive thy Church, beginning with me'; the Christian may equally wisely pray: 'Lord, bring in thy Kingdom, beginning with me.' The Kingdom involves the individual acceptance of the will of God. Therefore, to pray, 'Thy Kingdom come,' is to pray, 'Lord, help me to do your will.'

This is made even clearer when we look at two parallel New Testament passages. In Mark 9.43 we read:

> If your hand causes you to sin, cut it off; it is better for you *to enter into life* maimed than with two hands to go to hell.

In Mark 9.47 we read:

> If your eye causes you to sin, pluck it out; it is better for you *to enter the Kingdom of God* with one eye than with two eyes to be thrown into hell.

In these two passages *life* and *the Kingdom* are one and the same thing. We only find life in obedience to God. In doing his will we find our peace. Only in the Kingdom is there life, because clearly life is what it was meant to be only when it is lived in obedience to the will of God.

When we realize the indissoluble connection between the Kingdom and the will of God and life, then a whole series of New Testament passages and pictures and ideas fall into place.

(i) In view of this it is entirely natural that the Kingdom of God should *begin with an invitation*. It begins with the personal invitation of God to every man to accept his will, as that will is known in Jesus Christ. It may therefore be pictured as a feast and a banquet to which the host issues invitations, which the guests can accept or refuse to their glory or their shame (Matthew 22.1–14; Luke 14.16–24). To enter the Kingdom is to accept the invitation of God to be his guest, and a guest must always accept the laws and rules of the family into which he enters.

(ii) This is why *the Kingdom of God and repentance go hand in hand*. The initial message of Jesus was a summons to repent because God was about to begin his reign (Mark 1.14; Matthew 4.17). Repentance is literally *a change of mind (metanoia)*; and conversion is literally *a turning round and a facing in the opposite direction*. The instinctive human relationship to life is to make our own will, wishes and desires the dominating and moving force in life. When a man enters the Kingdom he has that change of mind which makes him stop obeying his own will and begin accepting God's will, which makes him stop looking at himself and start looking at God. A Christian is a man who has accepted the fact that he can never again do what he likes; and that he must for ever after do what God likes. The Christian life begins for a man, the entry to the Kingdom begins for him, when like Paul on the Damascus road, his one question is: 'What shall I do, Lord?' (Acts 22.10).

(iii) This is why the Kingdom of God necessarily starts from the smallest beginnings. Men do not enter the Kingdom in crowds; they must enter as individuals; for the moment of entry is the personal and individual acceptance of the will of God. That is why the growth of the mustard seed, the smallest of all seeds, into a tree symbolizes the Kingdom (Matthew 13.31, 32). That is why, if a man is placed in an environment which is hostile or indifferent to the claims of God, he must not regard it as something to regret and resent, but as a privilege and a challenge to be the tiny seed from which the Kingdom grows.

(iv) This explains why a man can be *not far from the Kingdom*. Jesus told the wise and instructed Scribe that he was not far from the Kingdom (Mark 12.28–34). A man can be in a position when he knows the will of God, and when he at least partly desires to accept it, but when he trembles on the brink of the great submission. And that is exactly why one of the barriers to the Kingdom is the inability to make a clear-cut decision. 'No one', said Jesus to the would-be follower, 'who puts his hand to the plough and looks back is fit for the Kingdom of God' (Luke 9.61, 62). There cannot be anything like a benevolent neutrality to the Kingdom of God. We may be on the very brink of it, but we cannot be in it until we make what may even be the surgical decision to accept the will of God.

(v) This explains why the situation which the challenge of the Kingdom creates is *necessarily a mixture*. More than one parable of Jesus makes exactly that point. The wheat and the tares grow together (Matthew 13.24–30). The dragnet brings in all sorts of things (Matthew 13.47). If the entry to the Kingdom and the acceptance of the will of God are one and the same, then there can be all sorts of reactions to the demand of the Kingdom. There may be blunt and deliberate rejection of the will of God. There may be a wistful yearning to accept it and yet an inability to make the necessary submission. There may be different levels of acceptance ranging from a tentative and timorous acceptance of the will of God to a gallant and adventurous total commitment to it. The mixture of the human situation is something which is inherent in the human situation in its relationship to God and his will.

(vi) It is exactly here that there lies *the difference* in the idea of the Kingdom which Jesus brought to men. 'My kingship', said Jesus to Pilate, 'is not of this world' (John 18.36). The Jews saw the Kingdom in terms of material prosperity, in terms of political power, in terms of national greatness. In the Kingdom of God they expected the world to be luxuriant with new beauty and new plenty; they expected the Jews at last to take their place in world leadership. To this day it is not uncommon to interpret the Kingdom in terms of social reform and material blessings. True, these things are part of the Kingdom, but they are the *end* not the *beginning* of the Kingdom; they are not so much the Kingdom itself as the results of the Kingdom. 'My Kingdom is within (or, among) you,' Jesus said (Luke 17.21). Jesus was quite clear that the initial change must come in people, for, if it did not, any new situation would simply relapse into the old all over again. The different demand that Jesus made was that the individual person must accept the will of God before there could be any change in society at all. The Kingdom must come in the hearts of men before the Kingdom could even begin to come in the world at large.

There is still much to say about the individual and the Kingdom, but we have arrived at the basic truth that to be in the Kingdom and to accept and do the will of God are one and the same thing, and they are the only thing which leads to life as God meant it to be. It is in light of this basic truth that we must understand a group of sayings of Jesus which stress the intensity of the effort necessary to enter the Kingdom.

(i) To enter the Kingdom of God is *worth any effort*. Jesus said: 'Seek first his Kingdom and his righteousness' (Matthew 6.33), and this has been well translated: 'Make the Kingdom of God the object of all your endeavour.' Luke and Matthew both have their own versions of a difficult saying of Jesus. In Luke 16.16 we read: 'The Law and the prophets were until John; since then the good news of the Kingdom of God is preached, and everyone enters it violently (AV, everyone presseth into it).' The word used for *entering violently* or *pressing into* is *biazesthai*, which is the word used of an army storming a city in a desperate attempt to gain an entry. Matthew repeats this saying: 'From the days of John the Baptist until now the Kingdom of Heaven has suffered violence, and men of violence take it by force' (Matthew 11.12). It is possible, especially in its Matthew version, that this saying refers to the violent persecution and attack that the Kingdom has suffered; but it is more likely, especially in its Luke version, that this saying has the idea of men storming their way into the Kingdom as valorous troops would storm their way into a city. 'The Kingdom of Heaven,' Denny somewhere writes, 'is not for the well-meaning but for the desperate.' The dilettante Christian will never gain entry into the Kingdom. The Kingdom is for those who are desperately in earnest. We need look no further than the tragic drama of Gethsemane to see how hard it was even for Jesus to accept the will of God and to act on it. Quite simply the meaning is: It is worth any effort, it is worth any agony, it is worth any blood and sweat and tears to do the will of God, and therefore to be a citizen and member of the Kingdom.

(ii) The Kingdom of God is worth *any price*. Jesus told the twin parables of the treasure hid in the field and the pearl of great price (Matthew 13.44–46). In both cases the discoverer of the treasure gave his all to become the possessor of the treasure. It may well be that in order to become a member of the Kingdom and in order to do the will of God a man may have to pay a costly price. He may have to sacrifice an ease and comfort that he might have enjoyed. He may have to lay aside a personal ambition which he might well have attained. He may have to sacrifice even the nearest and dearest personal relationships, for Jesus demanded that loyalty to him should exceed even the loyalties to kith and kin which are at the very heart of human life (Matthew 10.37; Luke 14.26). The meaning is that there is no price too high to pay to be a member of the Kingdom and to do the will of God.

(iii) To enter the Kingdom of God is worth *any sacrifice*. The hand, the eye, the foot which are liable to become a cause of sin have to be torn out and cut off and thrown away (Matthew 10.29, 30). No sacrifice is too radical and too surgical to make, if it is the price of entering the Kingdom and doing the will of God.

Before we leave this side of the matter, there are certain things to be said.

This is the necessary corrective to the idea that the only kind of Christianity is that kind of Christianity which is pictured as serenely and unquestioningly accepting the will of God. If Christianity must be like that, then in all reverence we must say that Jesus Christ did not possess it, for Jesus Christ sweated blood in the Garden in the agony of the battle to accept the will of God. There is little credit in doing that which is no effort to do or in winning a bloodless victory against a phantom enemy. Let no man be ashamed when he has to battle terribly to accept the will of God for himself; he is walking the way his Master trod. The shame is not in the battle, but in losing the battle.

But it remains to be said in this matter that God will be in no man's debt. If the battle is bitter, the reward of victory is great. Whatever sacrifice a man makes, it will be repaid to him a hundredfold (Luke 18.29; Mark 10.28–30; Matthew 19.27–30). The struggle is not for nothing and therefore it can be faced with gallantry and joy.

We now turn to the qualifications which fit a man to enter the Kingdom. To begin with we find two such qualifications in the Beatitudes.

(i) The Kingdom and its blessings belong to *the poor in spirit* (Matthew 5.3). In Greek the word is *ptochos*, and it means, not only poor, but absolutely and completely *destitute*. It translates the Hebrew word *ani*, which describes the poor, humble man, who in his helplessness and his trouble has put his whole trust in God.

This then means that the Kingdom belongs to those who have recognized their own total destitution and who have put their whole trust in God. Entry to the Kingdom belongs to the man who humbly rests his poverty in God's wealth, his ignorance in God's wisdom, his sin in God's mercy, his moral failure and his battle with temptation in God's grace. It belongs to the man who recognizes the obligation to do the will of God, but who also recognizes his utter inability to do it without the help that God can give.

(ii) The Kingdom and its blessings belong to those who are persecuted for righteousness' sake (Matthew 5.10). The persecuted are clearly those who love God's will more than personal comfort, personal reputation, personal ambition, personal safety and security, more than even life itself. The threat which obedience to God will nowadays bring to most people is not that of the loss of life and liberty. But it may well be the threat of unpopularity, ridicule, loneliness, sacrifice for principle. H. G. Wells once said that the characteristic of this age was that in it the voice of our neighbour is for many of us far louder than the voice of God. For the man who would enter the Kingdom the voice of God must be the most compelling thing in the universe.

(iii) More than once Jesus lays it down that one of the supreme conditions of entry to the Kingdom is the possession of the childlike spirit (Matthew 18.2, 3; Mark 10.14, 15; Matthew 19.14; Luke 18.16, 17). The child has two great qualities – humility and trust. A normal child does not want prominence, place and prestige. A normal child never doubts that his home will be there waiting for him; he will set out on a journey with his parents on which he does not know the way and on which he can pay for nothing in perfect trust. Humility and trust are the passports to the Kingdom.

(iv) There is a puzzling passage in the Sermon on the Mount in Matthew 5.17–20. There Jesus stresses the Law; not a letter and not the smallest part of a letter of it will ever become invalid. Anyone who relaxes its demands has but a low place in the Kingdom. 'I tell you, unless your righteousness exceeds that of the Scribes and Pharisees, you will never enter the Kingdom of Heaven.' What is the meaning of this?

The meaning is that he who enters into membership of the Kingdom is on a harder assignment than ever a Scribe or a Pharisee was. The Scribes and the Pharisees based life on the obedience to law. Now the very characteristic of law is that it is possible to satisfy it. When a man has done that which the law requires, when he has paid his just and lawful debts, when he has tholed his assize, in the Scots phrase, when he has stood his trial and paid his penalty, the law has no more claim on him. But the characteristic of life in the Kingdom is that its law is love, and the characteristic of love is that no man can ever satisfy its demands. No man has ever loved unless he has felt that, even if he gave his loved one the sun and the moon and the stars, it would not be enough. To be loved is to be placed in a debt which it is beyond the wit and power of man ever to pay. The obligation that is laid on the Christian is an obligation that no Scribe or Pharisee ever even glimpsed. The law of the Kingdom is love, and therefore the responsibility of the member of the Kingdom to God and to his fellowmen is without limit.

Just as there are certain qualifications of entry to the Kingdom, there are also certain barriers to entry to the Kingdom.

(i) *Lip service* debars a man from entry to the Kingdom. It is not the man who says Lord, Lord, who will enter the Kingdom but the man who does the will of God (Matthew 7.21). Profession without practice is maybe one of the commonest of all faults within the Church. One of the prayers written for the Lambeth Conference of 1948 runs as follows:

Almighty God, give us grace to be not only hearers but doers of thy holy word, not only to admire but to obey thy doctrine, not only to profess but to practise thy religion, not only to love but to live thy gospel. So grant that what we learn of thy glory we may receive into our hearts and show forth in our lives.

That indeed is the way to the Kingdom.

(ii) *The unforgiving spirit* debars a man from the Kingdom. Jesus makes this quite clear in the parable of the unforgiving debtor (Matthew 18.23–35). A merciless man can have no fellowship with the merciful God. A heart of hatred has automatically shut itself to the love of God. A man who will not forgive cannot enter into the presence of the God whose one desire it is to forgive. He who would be forgiven must learn to forgive. There is no place in the Kingdom for any man who in his heart nourishes a grudge against a fellowman and who in his life has an unhealed breach between himself and another.

(iii) Riches make entry into the Kingdom very difficult. Jesus said: 'Truly I say to you, it will be hard for a rich man to enter the Kingdom of Heaven. Again I tell you, it is easier for a camel to go through the eye of a needle than for a rich man to enter the Kingdom of God' (Matthew 19.23, 24; Mark 10.23–27; Luke 18.24, 25). Why? There are two main reasons.

First, the possession of many material things tends to fix a man's interests and thoughts to this world. He has so large a stake in this world that he can scarcely lift his eyes beyond it. Dr Johnson made his famous remark to Boswell after leaving the castle and policies of a great nobleman: 'Ah, Boswell, these are the things which make it difficult to die.' It is possible for a man to get so involved in this world that he forgets that there is any other.

Second, riches can become what someone has called 'a rival salvation'. They tend to give a false sense of security; they tend to make a man think that he can buy his way into and out of anything. They tend to make a man think that he can very well cope with life himself, and to make him forget God.

Jesus never said that riches debarred a man from the Kingdom, but he did say that they made entry to the Kingdom very difficult, for they tend to make a man forget that there is a Kingdom.

We may gather together, finally, certain remaining facts about the Kingdom.

The Kingdom involves the defeat of suffering, disease and death (Matthew 4.23; 10.1, 7, 8; 11.1–6; Mark 6.7; Luke 7.19–23; 9.11). It was Jesus' claim that if by the finger of God he cast out devils, the Kingdom had come (Matthew 12.28). The Kingdom of God is necessarily the defeat of evil and its power.

The Kingdom is universal. The gospel of the Kingdom will be preached in all the world (Matthew 24.14), and they will come from the north and the south and the east and the west to sit down in the Kingdom (Matthew 8.11; Luke 13.29). There are no racial distinctions, there are no most favoured nations, there are no *herrenvolk* in the Kingdom of God.

The Kingdom of God will come. Secretly, silently, but unstoppably the seed grows (Mark 4.26–29). Man can delay the Kingdom and man can hinder the Kingdom, but in the end the Kingdom will come.

The growth is not a growth which is infinite and unending; it is a growth which moves to a consummation. The Kingdom begins in time, but it has an end when eternity will finally break in upon time and when the kingdoms of the world will become the Kingdom of the Lord and of his Christ.

Thy Kingdom come – what a petition this is! It is not simply a petition that something will happen to the world of which we as it were will be spectators. It is a prayer that we should accept the will of God; that we should pay the price of that acceptance; that we should cleanse life of all that hinders that acceptance; that we should get to ourselves the things which are the passports to the Kingdom. No man need pray this prayer unless he is prepared to hand himself over to the grace of God in order that that grace may make him a new creature. This is no prayer for the man who desires to stay the way he is.

# CHAPTER FIVE

# Thy Will be Done

It might well be said that 'Thy will be done' is not only one of the petitions that Jesus taught his disciples to pray, but that it is also the centre, the key-note, and the ruling principle of Jesus' own life. Especially in the Fourth Gospel Jesus is represented as the One who came into the world for no other purpose than to do the will of God.

The disciples left Jesus tired at the well of Sychar in Samaria to go into the village to buy food. When they returned, they found that he did not wish to eat. They wondered if someone else had brought him food, but he said to them: 'My food is to do the will of him who sent me, and to accomplish his work' (John 4.31–34). 'I seek not my own will,' he said, 'but the will of him who sent me' (John 5.30). 'I have come down from heaven,' he said, 'not to do my own will, but the will of him who sent me' (John 6.38). And this reaches its unsurpassable peak in Gethsemane, where Jesus ends his prayer with the words of perfect submission: 'Nevertheless, not as I will, but as thou wilt' (Matthew 26.39). 'Thy will be done' (Matthew 26.42). But to this we will return.

Such an attitude to life is wholly in keeping with all that was highest and best in Jewish religion. The greatest thing in all the world for the Jew was the *Torah*, the Law, the instruction of God. Clearly, the obverse of law is obedience; and for a Jew life's greatest duty and life's greatest privilege was obedience to the Law. And it must always be remembered that the Jewish attitude to the Law was not the attitude of one who obeys because he is afraid of the consequences if he does not; it was not the attitude of one to whom obedience is a wearisome and burdensome and irksome obligation and necessity; it was the attitude of the lover whose greatest joy on earth it is to seek to obey the least behest of his loved one.

We have, for instance, only to read Psalm 119 to see the Jew's throbbing delight in obedience to God. 'Make me to understand the way of thy precepts.... I have chosen the way of faithfulness; I set thy ordinances before me.... I will run in the way of thy commandments.... Teach me, O Lord, the way of thy statutes; and I will keep it to the end' (verses 27, 30, 32, 33). 'I will find my delight in thy commandments.... Thy statutes have been my songs' (verses 47 and 54). 'I will never forget thy precepts; for by them thou hast given me life.... Oh, how I love thy law!' (verses 93 and 97). 'I love thy commandments above gold, above fine gold' (verse 127). 'His delight is in the law of the Lord' (Psalm 1.2). We cannot fail to see how often the words *love* and *delight* occur. This was no servitude; so far from that it was liberty. 'I will keep thy law continually, for ever and ever; and I shall walk at liberty, for I have sought thy precepts' (Psalm 119.44, 45). Obedience to the will of God, as expressed in the Law of God, was for the Jew life's first duty, life's first privilege, life's first delight, and life's only way to true freedom.

It is this very fact which brings us to something which is at the very heart of this petition. The same statement can mean very different things – it can mean almost opposite things – according to the tone of voice in which it is spoken and the feeling in the heart out of which it comes. This petition, 'Thy will be done', can mean very different things; the tone of voice in which it is spoken, and the emotion which gave it birth make all the difference.

(i) It can be spoken in *bitter resentment*. It can be the statement of one who knows that there is no escape and that there is no other way, but who is filled with rebellious, angry, bitter resentment that it should be so. Life was hard for Beethoven. In particular, it was a terrible fate for one whose very soul was music that he should have to experience complete deafness. It is said that when they found him dead, his fists were clenched, as if he would strike God, and his lips were drawn back in a snarl, as if he would spit his defiance and his bitterness at God. There are many people who know quite well that they must accept the will of God, but who spend their life in bitter resentment that it should be so.

(ii)  It can be spoken in the tone of one who *resignedly accepts a situation, not so much in bitterness, as because there is nothing else to do but to admit defeat.* Julian was the Roman Emperor who tried to put the clock back. He tried to reverse the decision of Constantine that Christianity should be the religion of the Empire, and he tried to re-introduce the worship and the service and the ceremonies of the ancient gods. In the end he was mortally wounded in battle in the east. The historians tell how, when he lay bleeding to death, he took a handful of his blood and tossed it in the air, saying: 'You have conquered, O man of Galilee!' It was not so much that he submitted; it was rather that he wearily accepted defeat, because there was nothing else to do.

Thomas Carlyle could say the bluntest things. He was told of a lavender-and-lace type of gushing lady who remarked that she accepted the world. 'By God,' commented Carlyle, 'she'd better!'

This is indeed acceptance of the will of God, but it is completely joyless; it is tired and weary and defeated and resigned, not content, still less glad, but only resigned to the fact that things must be so. There are many who live in a grey acceptance that things are as they are.

(iii)  It can be spoken in the tone of voice of one who *in the end accepts something, not exactly in weary resignation, but in the conviction that he cannot in any event do anything about it*, the tone of voice of one who yields with a more or less good grace to *force majeure*. In *Courage to Change*, her study of Reinhold Niebuhr, June Bingham tells a story which Niebuhr loved to tell. She relates how he wanted his daughter to come out for a walk, and she did not want to go. He extolled the virtues of exercise and fresh air, and in the end she came. As they ended their walk, he turned to her and said: 'Now aren't you glad that you decided to come?' Whereat his daughter replied: 'I didn't decide. You were just bigger!' Her philosophy was that it was better to do without a struggle what in the end you would be compelled to do anyway! There are some people who accept the will of God just because God is 'bigger'. They are not particularly resentful; and they are not particularly defeated and resigned; but equally they have no thrill and throb of joy in making God's will their choice. They could never say 'Oh, how I *love* thy law!'

(iv) It can be spoken in a tone of *serene and trustful love and joy and peace*. It can be spoken in the tone of one who is quite sure that 'a father's hand will never cause his child a needless tear'. In the days of the Covenanters terrible things happened in Scotland, as the government by the most savage measures tried to crush the Covenanters out of existence. Richard Cameron was one of the most famous and one of the greatest of them. They captured Richard Cameron's son. The son had notably beautiful hands. They cut off the hands and sent them to the father with a kind of wanton cruelty. Richard Cameron recognized them at once. 'They are my son's,' he said, 'my own dear son's. It is the Lord's will and good is the will of the Lord. He has never wronged me or mine.' Here is the complete and trusting acceptance of anything that might or could happen, as part of the will of God. As we shall see, there is something more to be said about things like that. But here is neither resentment, nor defeatedness, nor even acceptance; here there is the determination never to doubt the will of God.

Clearly, one question presents itself to be asked – Why is it that we find it so difficult to accept the will of God, and to say: 'Thy will be done'? It may well be said that there is one basic sin from which all other sins spring, and that basic sin is the sin of pride. The root reason why we find it so difficult to accept the will of God is that we so often in our heart of hearts think that we know better than God. We really believe that, if we could only get our way, we would be happy, that, if we could only arrange life and the events of life to suit our ideas, everything would be all right. That is why so many people would really rather pray, 'Thy will be *changed*' than, 'Thy will be *done*'. So long as there is pride and self-will in our hearts we cannot pray this petition, for the simple reason that we do not want to say it, because, whether we admit it or not, we would much prefer our own way, and we think our own way is better. That is one reason for reminding ourselves again and again what God is really like. There are two things in God which, if we really believe them, should make it easy to pray this prayer.

(i) We believe in the *wisdom* of God. We believe that God in his wisdom knows far better than we do what is for our ultimate good. We believe that only God sees all time. In the nature of things we must live in the moment. The past is past and cannot be recalled; we cannot see even a moment ahead. God alone can see the whole pattern of life, and, therefore, God alone can see what is to our ultimate good.

Long before Christianity ever entered this world the Stoics held this point of view. They held, not that God is *Eimarmene*, Fate, but that God is *Pronoia*, Providence. They believed that there was literally absolutely nothing in this world that happened outside the will of God, and that every action and motion of that will was directed towards the good of man. The Stoics could, therefore, say the noblest things. 'I have trained myself,' said Seneca, 'not merely to obey God, but to agree with his decisions.

I follow him because my soul wills it, and not because I must' (*Letters* 96.2). 'Use me henceforth for whatever thou wilt,' prayed Epictetus. 'I am thine; I crave exemption from nothing that seems good in thy sight; where thou wilt, lead me; in what thou wilt, clothe me' (*Discourses* 2.16.42). ' I have submitted my freedom of choice to God. He wills that I should have fever; it is my will too. He wills that I should get something; it is my will too. He does not will it; I do not wish it' (*Discourses* 4.1.89).

The Stoics went on to argue that if everything without exception in this world is the result of the will of God, then acceptance is the way to happiness and to freedom. Things cannot be changed. Therefore, to accept the will of God is to put yourself in line with the whole universe; to refuse the will of God is to batter your head against the walls of the universe, and, therefore, necessarily to be wretched and unhappy. *Deo parere libertas est,* said Seneca in the famous phrase (*On the Happy Life* 15.7). To obey God is perfect freedom. In the famous line of the Hymn of Cleanthes, as Seneca quotes it: '*Ducunt volentes fata, nolentem trahunt*' (*Letters* 107.11). Fate leads the willing, but drags the unwilling.

If a heathen can say this, if a man can say this who knows nothing of God in Jesus Christ, how much more should a Christian be able to say it? We may begin by making it our rule to remember always and ever the perfect wisdom of God.

(ii) We believe in the *love* of God. Now it is just here that we part company with the Stoics. The Stoic believed that literally everything is in accordance with the will of God, more, that it *is* the will of God. The Stoic then went on to say that a man must teach himself not to care what happened to anyone or to himself or to anything he had, because whatever happened was the will of God. Begin with a broken cup; go on to a torn robe; proceed to the death of a horse or a pet animal; and in the end you will be able to stand and watch your nearest and dearest die, and say,

'I don't care, I will not care,' for this is the will of God (Epictetus, *Discourses* 1.4.111, 112). Here is something which the Christian cannot and must not say.

Nothing has done the Christian faith and the Church more harm than the indiscriminate and blasphemous use of the phrase, 'It is God's will'. There are people who will go into a home in which a child has been killed in a street accident, in which a young life has been cut off before it has ever had time to blossom, in which a man or a woman is suffering agonies from some disease that not all the skill of man can help, in which untimely death has reft a mother from her children or a father from the family which was dependent on him, and who will say, 'It is God's will.' There are those who will hear of a terrible accident on the road, at sea, or in the air, or from some cataclysm in nature and who will say, 'It is God's will'. Such things are not the will of God. It is not God's will ever that a child should be needlessly killed by some reckless or drunken fool in a motor car, or that someone should be agonized by some disease which is the enemy of life. This is the direct opposite of the will of God; *this is the result of the sin of man*, not necessarily the sin of the sufferer, but the sin of the human situation of which the sufferer is a part. It is precisely such pain and sorrow and suffering that Jesus came to defeat, as his healing and miraculous powers show. It is a blasphemous slander on God to attribute to him acts and situations and events which, if we believe in the love of God in Jesus Christ, are the exact opposite of his will.

It may be the will of God – it often is – that we have to take some heart-breaking decision, that we have to accept some poignant disappointment, that we have to make some agonizing sacrifice, that we have to face some way from which our whole being shrinks. It is at such a moment as that, that we must be quite sure of the wise and loving will of God, no matter what it feels like.

But in these moments of human sin and agony and human sorrow, what *do* we say? We have to say: 'This is not God's will. This is the result in some way of the sin and the folly of man. You have been bitterly involved in this. God did not send it to you. But God can bring you through it, still erect, still steady-eyed, and still on your own two feet. And more, much more, out of this bitter thing you can come stronger, and purer, and nearer God and better able to help men, than ever you were before. For God can work for good even things that are outside his will, to those who trust and love him.' We can say: 'If you will allow God to use this and to use you, this, even this, can *become* part of his will.'

My mother died of cancer of the spine in such a way and out of such a pain that it was a relief to see her release. She was a saint, and the sorrow was very sore. But I can remember my father coming to me to this day and saying to me: 'You will have a new note in your preaching now.' And it was so, in the goodness of God, because I was better able to help others who were going through it, because I had gone through it.

(iii) So this brings us to the final thing about this petition. When we pray, 'Thy will be done', it does not mean that we either wish or expect to be saved from trouble. Here is the lesson of Gethsemane (Matthew 26.34–46). Jesus prayed to be released from his ordeal, but only, if it should be the will of God. He was not released; but he was given the power to go through it. When we pray, 'Thy will be done', we are not praying for release; we are not praying for resignation; we are praying for triumph. We are praying not to be taken out of a situation, but to be enabled to face it and conquer it and defeat it.

One of the greatest stories in the Bible is the story of Shadrach, Meshach and Abednego. They were threatened with death in the fiery furnace. Their answer was:

'If it be so, our God whom we serve is able to deliver us from the burning fiery furnace; and he will deliver us out of your hand,

O king. *But, if not,* be it known to you, O king, we will not serve your gods' (Daniel 3.16–18). *But, if not* – they did not look for escape, they looked for power to face this situation, whatever be the outcome.

The fact of life is quite simple. When the will of God insists that we face some difficult and sore and even agonizing situation, there is nothing to stop us running away from it. Jesus could have turned back in Gethsemane. But, if we do run away from it, there can be no happiness in life, for there can be no happiness when a man cannot face either himself or God any longer. But if we do face it, with all it demands, then in life there is a peace and a joy and a satisfaction that nothing else can give. That is why Plato long ago said that the wise man will always prefer to suffer wrong rather than to do wrong, and that is why the whole lesson of the Book of the Revelation is that there is all the difference in the world between *life* and *existence*, and that it may be that, if a man chooses to continue to *exist*, he may well forfeit *life*. To us the choice will not be between life and death, but it may be the choice between comfort and struggle, between ease and sacrifice; and it may well be that if we choose *pleasure*, we shall lose *joy*, for joy is the product of obedience to the will of God.

And how do we attain to this perfect obedience? The Stoics used to say that it was no more than a matter of the will. 'Bend your will to it, man,' they said, 'and you can do it.' A man learns to walk by practising walking and to read by practising reading. You can be good by practising goodness, and obedient by practising obedience. We know only too well that there is more to it than that. We know only too well that the human will at best is weak. We can only attain to this submission and loving obedience when we receive Jesus Christ into our hearts, and then he will give us the dynamic to say, as he himself said, 'Thy will be done.'

# CHAPTER SIX

# Give Us This Day Our Daily Bread

It might well be thought that this is the one petition in the Lord's Prayer about the interpretation of which there could be no argument and no dispute. But any such conclusion would be very far from the truth. It would almost be true to say that this petition is the petition about the meaning of which there is most doubt.

In the first place, there is doubt as to the actual meaning of it. This doubt becomes quite obvious, if we look at the various translations of it which have been offered by different translators.

It may be said that the translation of the AV, 'Give us this day our daily bread', is the standard translation. This is the translation of Tyndale, the Great Bible, the Geneva Bible, the Bishops' Bible of the older translations. It is the translation of the RV, the RSV and of the New English Bible; but the RV notes in the margin an alternative translation, 'our bread for the coming day', and the New English Bible gives as an alternative, 'our bread for the morrow'. On the whole it may be said that all these translations go right back to the Old Latin version of the Bible, which existed long before the Vulgate, and which had in it the phrase *quotidianum panem*, which is literally daily bread.

There is a group of translations all of which are closely connected with this standard translation, and which are variations on it, or slight improvements of it. Weymouth has: 'Give us today bread for the day'. Moffatt has: 'Give us today our bread for tomorrow'. Goodspeed has: 'Give us today bread for the day'. But there are two other different lines of translation.

The first line is represented by the Twentieth Century New Testament which has 'Give us today the bread that we shall need', and by E. V. Rieu who has, 'Give us the bread of life today'.

The second line goes back to the Vulgate, and is therefore of very great importance because the Vulgate is the Bible of the Roman Catholic Church. When in the fifth century Jerome produced the Vulgate by a revision of the Old Latin translation he did not keep the phrase *quotidianum panem*; he introduced a much more difficult phrase, *supersubstantialem panem*, super-substantial bread, which must mean bread of more than human, more than physical, more than material, more than earthly substance. This very naturally got into the Roman Catholic translations such as the Rheims. Equally naturally, this was the translation of Wicliffe, because Wicliffe was largely dependent on the Vulgate. He has, 'Give us this day our bread over other substance'. Ronald Knox in his modern Roman Catholic translation put into the text the standard translation, 'Give us this day our daily bread'; but he has a footnote saying that here the word in the Latin is *supersubstantialis*, which, he rightly says, has sometimes been taken as a direct reference to the Holy Eucharist.

Here then is the situation. Upon investigation the simple word *daily* produces a crop of complications. Why should this be so?

The reason for the doubt is this. The Greek word in question is *epiousios*; and the fact is that there is no other occurrence of it in the whole of Greek literature. This is the sole occurrence of the word; it may well have been coined by the man who wrote Matthew's Gospel; and therefore there is no parallel whatsoever which might help us to define its meaning. This statement needs to be slightly – and tantalizingly – qualified. The most valuable aid to the definition of New Testament vocabulary is the help of the papyri, these everyday Greek documents like letters and accounts and legal documents in which we find the Greek of the common people contemporary with the new Testament. In the papyri this word did turn up once in the plural neuter form *ta epiousia*, which seems to mean the requirements for the day. It is actually on a list of things which might be a shopping list. The papyrus has of course been recorded (Preisigke, *Sammelbuch* 5224.20), but the tantalizing thing is that the original papyrus has been lost, and it is a tantalizing quirk of fortune that the one papyrus which contains this unique Greek word is no longer available for direct examination. But, even so, wherein does the doubt arise, and what is the trouble in defining the meaning of this word? The trouble lies in this. The word *epiousios* is a compound word. The first part of it is the preposition *epi*, which can mean for, towards, upon. The second part of the word is *ousios*. This is a participial form. Now there are two very common Greek verbs *einai*, to be, and *ienai*, to come or to go (the *i* is pronounced separately, *ee-en-ai*). The feminine present participle of *einai* is *ousa*, and the feminine present participle of *ienai* is *iousa*. There is only an *iota* of a difference. The question therefore is whether the preposition *epi* has been combined with the participle of the verb *to be*, and whether therefore *epiousios* has something to do with being, or, whether it has been combined with the participle of the verb *to come*, and whether therefore *epiousios* has something to do with that which is coming. The interpretations of *epiousios* therefore oscillate between the ideas of *being* and *coming*.

(i) If we take it that *epiousios* has to do with being, then we will get three main ideas.

First, the prayer may mean bread for our physical being, bread to keep us in being, to keep us alive, bread for our day to day needs.

Second, the prayer may mean bread for our essential being, for our spiritual being. This then will be a prayer for the 'supersubstantial' bread, the bread that is real, essential, spiritual bread for our spiritual nourishment and growth.

Third, it is just barely possible that we might take *epi* in the sense of *near*, a sense which it can have. It would then be a prayer for the bread which is near, the bread that lies to hand; and that presumably would be a prayer for the simple needs of life, for the things which are obtainable by all, as opposed to recondite luxuries. It would then be a prayer for the simple, basic needs of life.

(ii) If we take it that *epiousios* has the sense of coming, then the prayer will be for bread for the coming day. This meaning is made the more likely in that *he epiousa* is the Greek for the morrow, the coming day. *Hemera* is the Greek for day and the full phrase would be *he epiousa hemera*, but the *hemera* is regularly left to be understood.

We must now come to a decision. Which of the two lines is more likely?

It is not really doubtful that it is the second of the two lines which is the more likely. The two possibilities are that the word *epiousios* is a compound of *epi* + *ousa* or of *epi* + *iousa*. Now by the laws of Greek word formation if *epi* were combined with *ousa*, the *i* of the *epi* would be elided and the resultant word would be *epousa*; whereas if *epi* were combined with *iousa*, there being two *i*'s, one of them would remain. The conclusion then is that *epiousios* has to do with *coming*, and that therefore the phrase means *bread for the coming day*. If then the prayer is prayed in the morning, it will be a prayer for the needs of the day; if it is prayed in the evening, it will be a prayer for the needs of tomorrow.

We turn now to the meaning of the petition.

(i) It has been taken as a prayer for 'the Sacrament of Christ's Body which we receive daily' (Augustine, *The Sermon on the Mount* 2.7.25). Augustine tells us that in his time (the fifth century) the Communion was received in some places daily, in some places at certain intervals (*Sermons on John* 26.15; *Letter* 54, *To Ianuarius* 2). His own attitude was that it should be received daily. In an Easter

Sermon (*Sermon* 227) to the newly baptized members of his congregation he said: 'You should realize what you have received, what you will receive in the future, what you ought to receive daily.'

So, if that meaning be taken, then this is a prayer for the bread of the Sacrament taken in daily communion with Christ and with his people. It is to be noted that Augustine well knew that daily Communion was not the universal custom of the Church, and he did not claim that this was the only meaning of the petition, for if it were the only meaning then there would be large numbers of Christians who would be unable to pray it.

(ii)  It has been taken as a prayer for spiritual food, and in particular for the spiritual food of the word of God in Scripture. As Augustine says, it is a prayer for 'spiritual food, namely, the divine precepts which we are to think over and to put into practice each day' (*The Sermon on the Mount* 2.7.27). This would be as the hymn has it:

> Break thou the bread of life,
>     Dear Lord, to me,
> As thou didst break the loaves
>     Beside the sea;
> Beyond the sacred page
>     I seek thee, Lord,
> My spirit pants for thee,
>     O living word.

On this interpretation the idea would be that the spiritual life of man is starved and stunted, unless it is daily nourished by the word of God in Scripture in the Bible; it is a prayer that our minds and hearts should be daily enriched in growth by the study of the word of God and the meditation upon it.

(iii)  This very naturally brings us to the interpretation that this is a prayer for nothing less than and nothing other than

Christ himself. 'I am the Bread of Life,' Jesus said. 'He who comes to me shall never hunger, and he who believes in me shall never thirst' (John 6.35). Our daily bread is nothing less than Christ, the Bread of life. On this interpretation we would have the same picture as is in Matthew Arnold's poem 'East London':

> 'Twas August, and the fierce sun overhead
> Smote on the squalid streets of Bethnal Green,
> And the pale weaver, through his windows seen
> In Spitalfields, look'd thrice dispirited.
> I met a preacher there I knew, and said:
> 'Ill and o'er-worked, how fare you in this scene?'
> 'Bravely!' said he; 'for I of late have been
> Much cheer'd by thoughts of Christ, *the living bread.*'

And indeed it is truest of all that we cannot live without the strength and help which we can daily draw from Jesus Christ.

(iv) We need not for a moment deny that all these meanings may be in this petition. But we believe that the meaning of this petition is much simpler than any of these things. We believe that it is just what it says, that it is a petition for daily bread, a petition that God should give to us the simple, ordinary things which we daily need to keep body and soul together. It is in fact one of the most precious things in life that we can take the simple, ordinary things to God, that God is not only the God of the great world-shaking, epoch-making events, but that he is also the God who cares that his humblest child may have daily bread to eat.

If we take this petition in that simple sense, certain things emerge from it.

(i) We must note right at the beginning that we are taught to pray, not, Give *me my* daily bread, but, Give *us our* daily bread. 'A man', runs the Jewish saying, 'should always join himself with the community in his prayers.' The very use of the plural precludes all selfishness in prayer. One of the most tragic features of present day society is what one can only call an essential mutual disregard. It is characteristic of our age that one class of the community does not care what happens to another class so long as its needs are met, one trade in the community does not care what happens to other trades so long as its demands are met. Life is pervaded with essential selfishness.

But he who prays this petition by the very form of the words is committed to a life in which he cannot have too much while others have too little, a life in which a war on want and the determination to bring bread to the hungry become for him inescapable duties. The man who in praying this petition thinks only of his bread has no real conception of what the petition means.

(ii) The prayer is for our *daily* bread. It does not look fearfully into the distant future; it is content to take the present and to leave it in the hands of God. 'Don't worry about tomorrow,' Jesus said (Matthew 6.34). Take it a day at a time. Gregory of Nyssa in commenting on this passage says (*The Lord's Prayer, Sermon* 4): 'God says to you as it were: He who gives you the day will give you also the things necessary for the day.' 'Who causes the sun to rise?' he goes on. 'Who makes the darkness of the night to disappear? Who shows you the rays of light? Who revolves the sky so that the source of light is above the earth? Does he who gives you so great things need your help to supply for the needs of your body?' This is a petition which no man can pray, unless he is prepared to live a day at a time. As Newman had it in his hymn:

I do not ask to see
The distant scene, – one step enough for me.

Marcus Aurelius laid it down that all that any man possesses is the instant of time in which at the very moment he is; the past is past and cannot be recalled; the future is necessarily unknown; and in this prayer a man takes his moment, which is all he has, and rests it in the goodness and the mercy and the bounty of God.

(iii)  Gregory of Nyssa in the sermon which we have already quoted stresses the fact that the prayer is for *bread*. The truly Christian man does not pray for luxuries; what he prays for is the simple food which is enough for life. 'So we say to God: Give us bread. Not delicacies or riches, nor magnificent purple robes, golden ornaments or precious stones or silver dishes. Nor do we ask him for landed estates, or military commands, or political leadership. We pray neither for herds of horses and oxen or other cattle in great numbers, nor for a host of slaves. We do not say, give us a prominent position in assemblies or monuments and statues raised to us, nor silken robes and musicians at meals, nor any other thing by which the soul is estranged from the thought of God and higher things; no – but only bread !' We do not pray for luxuries in order that 'the stomach, this perpetual tax collector, may live daintily through all this.' He gives the advice: 'Cling only to what is necessary.' Immediately we go beyond that, desire and covetousness creep into life, and life is distracted and distressed. Immediately we want more than our neighbour and set our own luxury in the forefront life goes wrong. 'So someone must weep, his neighbour must sorrow, many who are deprived of their property must be miserable, in order that their tears may contribute to enhance the ostentatious display of his table.' It is the simple things, the things for which nature itself supplies the flavouring, for which we are to ask, and with which we must be content. The prayer is for the satisfaction of simple need, not for the service of selfish luxury.

(iv)  There can be few passages in the Bible which better illustrate the meaning of the word *Give* than this passage does. Jesus taught us to pray, Give us this day our daily bread; but, if we prayed this petition and then simply sat down with folded hands and waited, we would quite certainly starve. The food is not going to appear all ready-made on our tables; God is not going to spoon feed any man; prayer is never the easy way to get God to do for us what we can well do, and must certainly do for ourselves. What this prayer does teach is that apart from and without God there would be no such things as food at all. It is God alone who has the secret of life, and God alone has the gift of making living things. No man ever made a living and a growing thing. In the most literal sense all food comes from God. The scientist can construct a synthetic seed which will have exactly the same chemical analysis as a real seed; but there will be one all-important difference – the synthetic seed will not grow. This petition acknowledges in full man's dependence on God and man's debt to God.

But there is the other side of the matter. If we would have our food, we must work for it. If God's seed is to grow, man must till the ground and prepare the soil and care for it and tend it. God's giving and man's toiling must go hand in hand; and the more man toils, the more God opens his hand and pours out his gifts upon him.

To pray, Give us this day our daily bread, is at one and the same time to express our dependence on God, our trust in God, and to challenge ourselves to the effort and the toil which will bring the gifts of God to ourselves, and through us to our fellowmen.

Give us this day our daily bread – in praying this petition we in trust ask God to supply all the physical and the spiritual needs of this life, we commit ourselves to the service of our fellowmen, and we pledge ourselves to the effort of mind and of body which will make it possible for God to give us more and more that our own lives may be enriched and that through us God's gifts may be shared with others.

# CHAPTER SEVEN

# Forgiven and Forgiving

Forgive us our debts, as we forgive our debtors (Matthew 6.12 AV). It has been well pointed out that the position of this petition in the Lord's Prayer is peculiarly appropriate. As Plummer points out, *forgiving* follows immediately on the heels of *giving*. The previous petition asked God *to give* us our daily bread; this petition asks him *to forgive* us for our sins. Tertullian says: 'It is fitting that after contemplating the liberality of God we should likewise address his clemency' (*On Prayer* 7). It is the more fitting in that when we remember the richness and the bounty of God's mercy we are all the more shamed by the memory of how little we deserve it.

This is the only petition of the Lord's Prayer which has two distinct and equally used forms, and this is true of each half of it. At the moment we look only at the first half. Sometimes the first half is prayed in the form of the AV: 'Forgive us our *debts*, as we forgive our *debtors*.' Sometimes it is prayed in the form which in ancient translations appears only in Tyndale and in modern translations occurs only in Knox: 'Forgive us our *trespasses*, as we forgive them that *trespass* against us.' If we add to these two forms the form of the petition given in Luke's version of the prayer, we get still a third form: 'Forgive us our *sins*; for we also forgive everyone that is *indebted* to us' (Luke 11.4). And in this petition the New English Bible moves furthest from the traditional renderings: 'Forgive us *the wrong that we have done*, as we have forgiven *those who have wronged us*.' It will be well to begin by trying to define the meaning, and by trying to see the reasons for the divergent translations.

In the body of the prayer in Matthew 6.12 the word in question is *opheilemata* which is the plural of *opheilema*. *Opheilema* is a word with a wide range of meanings all grouped round one common and unchanging idea. It always denotes something which is owed, something which is due, something which it is a duty or an obligation to give or to pay. In other words, it means a debt in the widest sense of the term. At its narrowest it is a money debt; at its widest it is any moral or religious obligation which a man in duty must discharge.

*Opheilema* is rare in biblical language. In the New Testament it occurs only once (Romans 4.4), and in the Old Testament it occurs only once (Deuteronomy 24.10), and in both places it has the sense of a money debt. The corresponding verb is *opheilein*, which means to owe, and which can be used in all the senses of the English word *ought*. It occurs more than 30 times in the New Testament, 8 times in the sense of owing money, and 25 times in the sense of moral or religious obligation.

We may look at certain examples of *opheilema* in secular Greek to see the width of its meaning. In the papyri it is often used in business documents of financial debts. Thucydides uses it of the duty of repaying kindness received (2.40). Plato uses it of a child's obligation to pay the debt he owes to his parents (Laws 717B). Aristotle uses it of the kind of financial debt which in all normal circumstances must be repaid (*Nicomachean Ethics* 1165a 3). *Opheilema* is that which is owed, that which a man ought to give or to pay, that which it is a moral or religious duty to give. Forgive us, says this petition, for every failure in duty, for failure to render to God and to man that which we ought to have rendered, for the debt to God and to man which we owe and which we have failed to pay.

We now turn to Luke's version (11.4). Luke has it: Forgive us our sins.' The word that Luke uses is *hamartia*, which is the commonest of all Greek words for sin. *Hamartia* was not originally an ethical word; originally it meant quite simply *a missing of the mark*, as when a javelin, or an arrow, or a blow misses its mark. In this sense, sin is a failure to hit the mark, a failure to realize the true aim of life, a failure to be and to do that which we ought to have done, and which we could have been and could have done. It can seem that, though they are based on different pictures, *opheilema* and *hamartia* are not radically different in meaning.

It so happens that it is quite possible to explain why Matthew used the one and Luke the other. Jesus, of course, did not give the Lord's Prayer to his disciples in Greek; he gave it in Aramaic. Now in the time of Jesus in Palestine the rabbis thought of sin almost exclusively as a failure in obedience to God. To them goodness was obedience, sin was disobedience. This is to say that man's first obligation is to give God obedience; not to give obedience to God is to be in debt to God; and therefore their commonest word for sins was *choba'*, which in fact means *debt*. This is to say, that it would be quite correct to translate Matthew's *opheilemata* by the word *sins*, because it is exactly the Greek equivalent of the Aramaic *choba'*, which is literally a *debt*, but which is the commonest rabbinic word for *sin*. There is then no difference at all between Matthew and Luke; they are simply both translating the Aramaic *choba'*, and Matthew, being characteristically Jewish, chooses a Greek word meaning *debts*, while Luke, being characteristically Greek, uses a more general Greek word for sin.

This explains Matthew and Luke, and it also completely justifies the NEB rendering, but it still leaves the rendering *trespasses* unexplained. The truth is that linguistically speaking there is no justification whatever for the use of the word *trespasses* to render the Greek word *opheilemata*. How then did *trespasses* get into the text? As we have seen, its first appearance in the English

Bible is with Tyndale, and of the translators ancient and modern only Ronald Knox retained it. It may be that Tyndale inserted *trespasses* into the text of the prayer on the strength of the amplification in Matthew 6.14, 15 : 'For if ye forgive men their *trespasses*, your heavenly Father will also forgive you: but if ye forgive not men their *trespasses*, neither will your Father forgive your *trespasses*.' There the word in Greek is *paraptomata*, which means properly a false step, a slip, a blunder. It can, for instance, be used for a slip in grammar (Longinus, *On the Sublime* 36.2), and it could quite reasonably be translated *trespasses*. Although the words are different, it may be that Tyndale took the word into the prayer from the amplification. Why should he do so? It may well be that Tyndale did not wish to use the word *debts*, because there were those who desired to take this petition, 'Forgive us our debts, as we forgive our debtors', as a statement that debts in the money sense of the term are obliterated and need no longer be paid. Augustine (*The Sermon on the Mount* 2.8) in point of fact spends the greater part of his exposition of this petition dealing with the obviously not inconvenient interpretation which found in this petition a new way to abolish old debts.

From the purely linguistic point of view, in the text of the Lord's Prayer in this petition *debts* is a correct rendering, *trespasses* is not justifiable, and it may well be that *sins* would give the meaning most simply, most unmistakably, and not inaccurately.

We must now turn directly to the meaning and the interpretation.

(i) 'Pray then like this,' said Jesus; and one of the things which we are to pray is, 'Forgive us our debts.' Jesus bade all men to pray that prayer without distinction. He did not say that this is the prayer which sinners ought to pray; he said that this is the prayer that all men ought to pray.

That is the proof of the universality of sin. Luther commenting on this petition said: 'We must note how here again the indigence of our miserable life is indicated; we are in the land of debts, we are up to the ears in sin.' To ask forgiveness for sin is in itself a confession of sin. Tertullian said: 'A petition for pardon is itself a full confession, because he who begs for pardon fully admits his guilt' (*On Prayer* 7).

The Bible is never afraid to show its great men under the consciousness of sin. 'Depart from me,' Peter cried out to Jesus, 'for I am a sinful man' (Luke 5.8). 'Christ Jesus came into the world to save sinners,' said Paul. 'And I am the foremost of sinners' (1 Timothy 1.15). 'If we say we have no sin,' writes John, 'we deceive ourselves, and the truth is not in us. If we confess our sin, he is faithful and just, and will forgive us our sins and cleanse us from all unrighteousness' (1 John 1.8, 9). The people who are condemned are people like the Pharisee who contentedly thanked God that he was not as other men are, and certainly not like the tax-gatherer weeping for his sins (Luke 18.9–14). It is the young man who blandly claimed that he had kept all the commandments who went away sorrowful (Matthew 19.16–22; Mark 10.17–22; Luke 18.18–23).

The fact that Jesus taught all men to pray this prayer shows the universality of sin; and to pray this prayer a sense of sin is a prior requirement. This therefore is an impossible prayer for a generation which, in the famous phrase of Sir Oliver Lodge, is not worrying about its sins. Since then there can be no asking for forgiveness without the consciousness of sin, it may well be said that to be conscious of no sin is the greatest sin of all.

Origen (*On Prayer* 28.1–5), in order to awaken the sense of sin, enumerates the debts which every man owes simply because he is a man. He uses the famous threefold classification. *A man owes a debt to his fellowman.* He owes a debt to his fellow-christians, to his fellow-citizens, and to all men. He owes a debt to strangers, to the aged, to those of his own family such as his sons and his brothers. There is in life a whole series of 'obligations, contracted through the spirit of wisdom, and bound to issue in charity'. *A man owes a debt to himself.* He owes a debt to his body, not to waste its strength and health in injuring pleasure. He owes a debt to his mind, to use it in such a way that it retains its keenness. He owes a debt to his soul, for he must tend his soul carefully. *A man owes a debt to God.* Because God made us in his image we must love him with heart and soul and mind and strength (Mark 12.30; Luke 10.27; Matthew 22.37). He owes a debt to Jesus Christ who purchased us at the price of his own blood (Acts 20.28; 1 Peter 1.18, 19; Revelation 5.9). He owes a debt to the Holy Spirit whom he must not grieve (Ephesians 4.30). Origen has the odd but lovely idea that a man owes a debt to the angel who looks after him and protects him (Matthew 18.10). Origen quotes 1 Corinthians 4.9, which says that we have become a spectacle to the world, to angels and to men. We are, he says, like actors in some great and crowded theatre who owe a debt to the spectators to act out the play as well as possible. Even so, we must play out the drama of life nobly for the sake of those who in heaven and upon earth look on. Apart from these general debts, we have debts to the widow and orphan, to the deacon, the priest and the bishop, and husband and wife owe a debt to each other (1 Corinthians 7.3, 5). 'While a man is alive,' says Origen, 'there is not a single hour, day or night, when he is not a debtor.' The very fact that we are set in the human situation has put us under a series of debts which no man can ever fully repay. A man in the nature of things is bound to be a defaulter, and therefore in the nature of things is bound to stand in need of forgiveness.

Gregory of Nyssa (*Sermons on the Lord's Prayer* 5) presses home on man his debt. Man owes a debt to God, because man has separated himself from his Maker, and deserted to the enemy, and has thus become a runaway and an apostate from his natural Master. Man has exchanged the liberty of free-will for the wicked slavery of sin and has preferred the tyranny of the power of destruction to the companionship of God. The very fact that man has gone his own way puts him in debt to God.

The very constitution of man makes him a sinner. Gregory of Nyssa has a curious interpretation of Jeremiah 9.21, which says that 'death is come in through the window.' The windows are the senses; it is through the senses that sin and therefore death gain an entry into life. Man in his very being is necessarily open to the invasion of sin.

Any man who honestly faces the human situation cannot be other than conscious of his debt, and of his need to pray to be forgiven.

(ii) When we examine the second part of this petition we find that there are two forms of it. The two forms are exemplified by the renderings of the AV and the RSV. The AV renders:

> Forgive us our debts as *we forgive* our debtors.

The RSV renders:

> Forgive us our debts as *we also have forgiven* our debtors.

In the first instance the verb is in the present tense; in the second it is in the past tense. We find the translations divided between these two forms. The present tense is the translation of all the older versions, Wicliffe, Tyndale, the Rheims, the Geneva, the Great Bible, the Bishops' Bible; of the modern translations Kingsley Williams and Ronald Knox retain the present. The majority of the modern translations have the past tense, E. V. Rieu, Weymouth, Moffatt, Goodspeed. The NEB renders:

> Forgive us the wrong we have done,
> As we have forgiven those who have wronged us.

The difference here is not due to a difference in the mind of the various translators; it is due to a variant reading in the Greek text. Certain manuscripts read the present tense (*aphiomen*), we forgive, and certain manuscripts read the perfect tense *aphekamen*, we have forgiven. On the whole, the better manuscripts read the past tense, and the more correct reading is, 'as we have forgiven.'

In point of actual meaning the variation makes no great difference. In the one case we ask God to forgive us as it is our practice to forgive other people; in the other we ask God to forgive us as we have in fact forgiven others before we make our own prayer.

There is a further question as to how we are to interpret the 'as'. Does the 'as' express *similarity* or *proportion*? Does the petition mean: 'Forgive us in the same way as we have forgiven others?' Or, does it mean: 'Forgive us in proportion as we have forgiven others?' There are two things which will help us to come to a decision. In Luke's version (Luke 11.4) there is no ambiguity. Luke's version reads with unimportant variations in all translations: 'Forgive us our sins; for we also forgive everyone that is indebted to us.' Or, as the NEB has it: 'Forgive us our sins for we too forgive all who have done us wrong.' In the Luke version we acknowledge that we have no right at all to pray for forgiveness for our own sins before we have forgiven those who have done us wrong. In it we come to God telling him that we have forgiven before we even ask for his forgiveness. The second thing which helps us is the expansion and amplification of this petition which follows the prayer: 'For if ye forgive men their trespasses, your heavenly Father will also forgive you; but if ye forgive not men their trespasses, neither will your Father forgive your trespasses' (Matthew 6.14, 15). Or, as the NEB has it: 'For if you forgive others the wrongs they have done, your heavenly Father will also forgive you; but if you do not forgive others, the wrongs you have done will not be forgiven by your Father' (Matthew 6.14, 15).

The variations in reading and the variations in meaning do not effectively alter the basic significance of the petition. No matter what the reading, and no matter what the precise meaning of the 'as', the basic fact is that there is the closest possible connection between human and divine forgiveness, and that he who is unforgiving has cut himself off from the forgiveness of God. However we take this petition we cannot evade the truth that to be forgiven we must be forgiving. And this presents us with a truth so challenging and even so threatening that we are not surprised to find that Chrysostom tells us that in his day there were many who suppressed this clause of the Lord's Prayer altogether.

The connection between human and divine forgiveness is deeply ingrained into New Testament thought. The parable of the unforgiving debtor clearly lays it down that an unforgiving man can hope for no forgiveness (Matthew 18.23–35). As a man judges others, so he will be judged himself, and in matters of mercy he will get what he gives (Matthew 7.1, 2; Mark 4.24; Luke 6.37, 38). It is the merciful who will receive mercy (Matthew 5.7). 'Judgement is without mercy to one who has shown no mercy' (James 2.13).

This was in fact a legacy of Jewish thought. The rabbinic teaching is full of the conviction that the merciful man will receive the mercy of God, and that the merciless man has cut himself off from the mercy of God. Gamaliel said: 'So long as you are merciful, God will have mercy upon you, and if you are not merciful, he will not be merciful to you.' Raba said: 'Whom does God forgive? Him who overlooks the transgressions of others.' 'So long as a man remains in his stiffness God does not forgive him.' 'Whenever you have pity God forgives you.' 'Learn to receive suffering, and to forgive those who insult you.' 'Even if a man pays compensation to another whom he has injured, he is not forgiven by God, till he seeks forgiveness from the man he has insulted.' And it is interesting to note that this saying goes on to lay it down, that if the injured party, when asked to do so, refuses to forgive, *he* is to be regarded as merciless. Rabbi Zutra's goodnight prayer before sleeping was: 'Forgiven is everyone who has done me an injury.' The Day of Atonement was the day on which the grand act of atonement for sins known and unknown, sins realized and sins unrealized, the total sin of the community was carried out in the Temple, and which continues to be observed by almost every Jew is this day. Yet it is laid down that the Day of Atonement is unavailing unless a man has appeased and sought the pardon of the neighbour whom he has wronged. Later Gregory of Nyssa was to say that a man's prayer for forgiveness cannot be heard when the voice of him whom he has wronged is drowning it (*Sermons on the Lord's Prayer* 5). Maybe the noblest statement of this is in The Wisdom of the Ben Sirach:

> He that takes vengeance will suffer from the Lord,
> and he will firmly establish his sins.
> Forgive your neighbour the wrong he has done,
> and then your sins will be pardoned when you pray.
> Does a man harbour anger against another,
> and yet seek for healing from the Lord?
> Does he have no mercy toward a man like himself,
> and yet pray for his own sins?
> If he himself, being flesh, maintains wrath,
> who will make expiation for his sins?
>
> (Ecclesiasticus 28.1–5)

Divine and human forgiveness are one and indivisible.

There is then no evading the principle that the condition of forgiveness is the forgiving spirit. Long ago Gregory of Nyssa (*Sermons on the Lord's Prayer* 5) pointed out that it could not be otherwise for the very simple and the very fundamental reason that there can be no fellowship between opposites. 'It is impossible that a wicked man should be intimate with a good man, or that someone wallowing in impure thoughts should be friends with someone who is perfectly pure. Thus a callous man trying to approach God is far from the divine charity.... Therefore it is absolutely necessary that a man who approaches the charity of God should rid himself of callousness.' It is impossible that a merciless man should have fellowship with the divine mercy, or a loveless man fellowship with the divine love, or an unforgiving man with the God whose name is Saviour and who delights to forgive. The very nature of God is such that between him and the unforgiving man there is a self-erected barrier.

(iii) It thus becomes clear that there is in this petition a certain danger. 'Forgive us our debts, as we forgive our debtors.' The petition asks God to forgive us as we forgive others. This can only mean that if we are unforgiving, if we pray this when we are in a state of bitterness towards a fellowman, we are deliberately asking God *not* to forgive us.

Luther connects this petition with the saying in the Psalms which says of the wicked man: 'Let his prayer be counted as sin!' (Psalms 109.7). When this prayer is prayed by a bitter and an unforgiving man it becomes a sin. 'Psalm 109.7 says his prayer will be a sin in the sight of God; for what else canst thou mean when thou sayest, "I will not forgive", and yet standest before God with thy Pater Noster, and babblest, "Forgive us our debts, as we forgive our debtors", than, "O God, I am thy debtor, and I also have a debtor; I am not willing to forgive him, therefore do thou also not forgive me: I will not obey thee though thou shouldst declare me pardoned; I would rather renounce thine heaven and everything else, and go to the devil"?' It is a dreadful thought that a man should ask God *not* to forgive him, and yet that is precisely what the unforgiving man does when he prays this prayer.

In the South Sea Islands in Tahiti it was Robert Louis Stevenson's custom to have family worship each day and in it to have the Lord's Prayer. One day in the middle of the prayer he rose from his knees and left the room. His wife hurried after him thinking that he was ill. 'What is the matter?' she said. ' Are you ill?' 'No,' he answered, 'but I am not fit to pray the Lord's Prayer today.' How often that must be true of all of us! Of all prayers the Lord's Prayer can least be used unthinkingly. Once General Oglethorpe remarked to John Wesley: 'I never forgive', whereat Wesley answered: 'Then I hope, sir, you never sin.'

A man has to examine himself before he dares to pray this prayer, for in this petition a man becomes nothing less than his own judge. As Chrysostom had it: 'God makes you arbiter of the judgement; as you judge yourself, so he will judge you.' Gregory of Nyssa (*Sermons on the Lord's Prayer* 5) writes: 'Be yourself your own judge; give yourself the sentence of acquittal. Do you want your debts to be forgiven by God? Forgive them yourself and God will ratify it. For your judgement of your neighbour, which is in your own power, whatever it may be, will call forth the corresponding judgement upon you. What you decide for yourself will be confirmed by the divine judgement.' This is only another instance of the universal rule that God's attitude to any man is determined by that man's attitude to his fellowmen. There is a very real sense in which we are every day engaged in judging ourselves.

(iv) There is one last comment on this clause of the Lord's Prayer which is the boldest and the most startling of all. It is again in the sermon of Gregory of Nyssa which we have already quoted. Gregory writes: 'Jesus wants your disposition to be a good example to God! We invite God to imitate us – "Do thou the same as I have done. Imitate thy servant, O Lord, though he be only a poor beggar, and thou art the King of the Universe. I have shown great mercy to my neighbour – imitate thy servant's charity, O Lord!" ' It is in fact the tremendous and audacious leap of this petition that it does ask God to treat us as we have treated others. We may hesitate to put the matter in so starkly startling a way as Gregory put it; but one fact remains. Forgiveness is the very prerogative of God. 'Who can forgive sins but God alone?'

asked the Jews. In this prayer there is laid upon us the duty of forgiving the sins of others. And this fact is for ever true, that a man is never closer and more kin to God than when he forgives a fellowman.

Forgive us our debts as we forgive our debtors – herein we confess our own sin, and herein we accept the fact that only the forgiving can be forgiven. Herein we follow the example of God. As Paul had it: 'Be kind to one another, tenderhearted, forgiving one another, as God in Christ forgave you' (Ephesians 4.32). A Jewish rabbi once said: 'He who hears himself cursed, and has the opportunity to stop the man who curses him, and yet keeps silence, makes himself a partner with God.' We are the disciples of him who prayed for forgiveness for those who were nailing him to a cross (Luke 23.34). If we would imitate our Lord, and if we would be kin to God, we must forgive, and he who forgives will find for himself the forgiveness of God.

# CHAPTER EIGHT

# The Ordeal of Temptation

Lead us not into temptation, but deliver us from evil (Matthew 6.13 AV). We may begin by noting that there are certain variations in the translation of this petition of the Lord's Prayer.

The petition falls into two clauses. First, Lead us not into temptation. This translation goes very far back and lasts right down into the modern translations. It is the translation of Wicliffe, Tyndale, the Great Bible, the Bishops' Bible. It is the translation of the Rheims and the Geneva Bibles with the un-important variation of *tentation* for *temptation*. It is the translation of Moffatt and Knox and of Kingsley Williams. The variations on this translation are in the word *Lead* and the word *temptation*. The Revised Version has: '*Bring* us not into temptation'. Rieu, Weymouth and the New English Bible all have the word bring instead of lead. Ferrar Fenton has: 'Let us not be led into tempta-tion.' E. J. Goodspeed has: 'Do not subject us to temptation.' C. C. Torrey, basing his translation on a hypothetical Aramaic original, has: 'Let us not yield to temptation.' Two modern trans-lations alter the word *temptation*. E. V. Rieu has: 'Do not bring us to *ordeal*.' And the New English Bible has: 'Do not bring us to the *test*.'

The second clause is, 'But deliver us from evil.' In this clause the renderings vary between *evil*, as a perfectly general term including all evil, and *the Evil One*, meaning Satan or the Devil, the personal power of evil. There is a real doubt here, and some of the translations which insert one of the two translations in the text have the other in the margin. *Evil*, as a general term, is the translation of Wicliffe, Tyndale, the Rheims, the Geneva, the Great Bible, the Bishops' Bible, the RSV (margin, the evil one), E.V. Rieu, Ferrar Fenton (that evil), Moffatt and Knox. *The Evil One*, in the sense of Satan, the Devil, is the translation of The Revised Version, Weymouth (margin, evil), Kingsley Williams, E. J. Goodspeed, and the New English Bible.

As we shall come to see, some of these variations are not unimportant in the task of tracking down the real significance of this petition.

It would be true to say that this is the most natural and instinctive petition in the Lord's Prayer. It is, says Chrysostom, the natural appeal of human weakness and human danger. And yet the odd fact is that this petition has involved more argument and more explanation than any other petition. It is perfectly true that when instinct gives place to reason this petition does involve us in puzzling questions. The difficulties are twofold.

(i) How can we reasonably pray not to be led into temptation when in point of fact temptation is so integral to human existence on earth that we cannot conceive of life without it? As Origen pointed out (*On Prayer* 29.5) the Septuagint (Greek) version of Job 7.1 can be translated: 'Is not man's life on earth one continuous temptation?' Origen goes on: 'Has anyone ever thought man to be beyond temptations of which he was aware from the day he attained to reason? Is there any time when a man is sure that he has not to struggle against sinning?' It is quite simply impossible to think of human existence without temptation.

Further, and, as we shall come to see this is of the first importance, in Greek the word *trial* and the word *temptation* are the same word (*peirasmos*); and again and again the Bible points out the supreme value of trial. 'When he has tried me,' said Job, 'I shall come forth as gold' (Job 23.10). 'Count it all joy, my brethren,' said James, 'when you meet various trials, for you know that the testing of your faith produces steadfastness' (James 1.2). ' In this', writes Peter, 'you rejoice, though now for a little while you may have to suffer various trials, so that the genuineness of your faith, more precious than gold which though perishable is tested by fire, may redound to praise and glory and honour at the revelation of Jesus Christ' (1 Peter 1.6, 7). In all these cases the word for trial is *peirasmos*, which is the very same word as is used for *temptation* in this clause of the Lord's Prayer.

The undoubted teaching of life is that life is inconceivable without temptation, and the undoubted teaching of Scripture is that, if temptation were removed from life something irreplaceable would be lost with it.

(ii) When we come to think of it, this is on the face of it an extraordinary prayer to pray, for in what sense can we ever believe that God would lead us into temptation? How could God ever be responsible for the attempt to seduce man into sin? As Tertullian (*On Prayer* 8) said: 'Far be the thought that the Lord should seem to tempt anyone, as if he were ignorant of the faith of any, or else were eager to overthrow it.' This is indeed a difficulty so acute that we are driven to examine more closely the meaning of the words of this petition in order to see if there is a meaning in it which our English versions find it difficult to express. Let us then examine the word which is rendered *temptation*.

The word which is rendered temptation is *peirasmos*. *Peirasmos* is a noun, and like all Greek nouns which end in *-asmos* it describes a process. It is common in biblical literature, but it is not common in secular literature, and we will get the basic idea which lies behind it and which lies behind this petition better, if we examine the verb with which it is connected. The verb is *peirazein*. It may be said that the Greek verb *peirazein* has all the many senses of the English verb *to try*.

(i) It can mean quite simply *to try* or *to attempt* to do something. So it is used in the sentence: 'They *attempted* to go into

Bithynia' (Acts 16.7). This use is not specially relevant for our investigation.

(ii) It regularly means *to test* or *to prove*. In this sense it can be used as exactly parallel to the verb *dokimazein*, which is the word for testing or proving the quality of a metal, the genuineness or otherwise of a coin. In this sense *peirazein* can be used, for instance, for the process of testing the effects of a drug by experiment in its use. It is said that when the Queen of Sheba heard of the wisdom of Solomon she came '*to test* him with hard questions' (1 Kings 10.1; cp. 2 Chronicles 9.1). It is said that the Church at Ephesus has *tested* those who claim to be apostles, and who are not, and has found them false (Revelation 2.2). 2 Corinthians 13.5 is a very good example of this: 'Examine (*peirazein*) yourselves, to see whether you are holding to your faith. *Test* yourselves (*dokimazein*).' *Peirazein* describes the process by which the genuineness of anything or anyone is tested, and thereby proved or disproved.

(iii) In the Bible *peirazein* is often used of God's testing of men to see whether or not their faith is genuine, loyal, and true. It is forbidden to listen to a false prophet or to a dreamer of dreams. When such a man emerges, 'The Lord your God is *testing* you to know whether you love the Lord your God with all your heart and with all your soul' (Deuteronomy 13.3). So God *tested* Abraham by seeming to demand the sacrifice of Isaac (Genesis 22.1). God does not allow us to be tested beyond that which we can bear (1 Corinthians 10.13).

This meaning is very important; it is the more important because in the AV *test* and *tempt* are used in the same sense, as they were in Elizabethan English. For instance, in Genesis 22.1 which we have already quoted the AV has, 'God did *tempt* Abraham'. It is clearly impossible to think of God trying to seduce Abraham into sinning; the meaning here is *test*. In point of fact, on at least twenty occasions the RSV alters an AV *tempt* into *test*.

*Peirazein* is regularly used of the divine placing of a man in a situation which is a test, a situation in which he *may* fall, but in which he is not *meant* to fall, a situation which *may* be his ruin, but out of which he is *meant* to emerge spiritually strengthened and enriched. It is used of a situation into which temptation to disloyalty certainly enters, but the characteristic of which is not so much temptation as it is testing.

(iv) *Peirazein* is frequently used in the New Testament of the action of men who maliciously cross-examine or otherwise test someone with the deliberate intention of catching him out or making him incriminate himself. In this sense it is repeatedly used of the Scribes and Pharisees asking Jesus questions which were designed to entrap him (Matthew 16.1; 19.3; 12.18).

(v) *Peirazein* is frequently used of the direct and deliberate seduction to sin which in English is the normal meaning of the word to tempt. Husbands and wives are not to deny each other their natural rights except by agreement, 'lest Satan tempt you through lack of self-control' (1 Corinthians 7.5). In this sense Satan is pre-eminently *ho peirazon*, the tempter. It is thus that the Devil tempted Jesus in the wilderness (Matthew 4.1–11).

In this last sense *peirazein* is a bad word, for the action in it is designed to lure a man into sin.

(vi) There is one last use of the word *peirazein* both in the Old and the New Testaments which is not strictly relevant for the purposes of our present investigation, but which for the sake of completeness we include. Frequently the Bible speaks of man tempting God (Exodus 17.2; Numbers 14.22; Isaiah 7.12; Matthew 4.7. Acts 15.10). The idea there is that a man tests God, in the sense of seeing how far he can go with God. He, as it were, tempts God to use his holy power; to put it in a colloquial phrase, he tries to see just how much he can get away with unpunished.

It can be seen that the word *peirasmos* is by no means easy to translate. It has in it three ideas. It has in it the simple idea of proving or testing the quality of a person or a thing. It has in it the idea of putting a person in a situation which is in reality a test but which involves the possibility of failure. And it has in it the idea of the deliberate invitation and seduction to sin. And the trouble about translating the word is that there is no one English word which does justice to the various ideas which reside in the word. The majority of the translations of this petition of the Lord's Prayer concentrate on the temptation side of the word. E.V. Rieu by using the word *ordeal*, and the NEB by using the word *test* concentrate almost entirely on the testing side of the word.

The English word which comes nearest to containing both ideas is the word *trial*; and it is significant to note that the RSV in at least eight instances substitutes the word *trial* for the AV *temptation* in the translation of the word *peirasmos*. So in Luke 22.28 Jesus speaks of the sharing of the disciples in his *trials*. Paul speaks to the Ephesian elders of the *trials* which befell him (Acts 20.19). In James 1.2 the RSV substitutes *various trials* for *divers temptations*, as it does in 1 Peter 1.6. Paul's physical condition is a *trial* to the Galatians, not a temptation (Galatians 4.14). The blessing is on the man who endures *trials*, rather than temptations (James 1.12). In 2 Peter 2.9 the RSV substitutes God knows 'how to rescue the godly from *trial*', for 'how to deliver the godly out of *temptation*'. In Revelation 3.10 the AV speaks of the hour of *temptation* which is coming on the world; the RSV speaks about the hour of *trial*; and the NEB of the *ordeal* that is to fall on the whole world. And in all these passages the rendering is greatly improved by the substitution of *trial* for *temptation*. A *peirasmos* is an event or situation which tries a man. It tries him in the sense that it is difficult to bear; and it tries him in the sense that his reaction to it shows what kind of a man he is.

From all this certain truths emerge in regard to the Christian conception of temptation. We may say three things about temptation.

(i) Temptation is universal and inescapable, part and parcel of the human situation. There is no man on earth who does not need to pray this petition.

(ii) Temptation is not outside the plan and the purpose of God. It is part of the structure of life and living which God uses to make life what he meant it to be. The ordeal of temptation is an integral factor in the making of manhood.

(iii) There is in temptation always an element of probation. Temptation is always essentially a test. Even when it is a seduction to sin, it is still a test of a man's resistance power.

It thus becomes true to say that temptation is not so much the penalty of manhood as it is the glory of manhood. It is that by which a man is made into the athlete of God.

(iv) To this we may add the fourth fact. The very fact that we pray this petition is the proof that we are well aware that we cannot deal with temptation by ourselves, but that we need the power which is not our own in order that we may emerge triumphantly from the test.

When we remember this biblical view of temptation, it is clear that our problem is considerably simplified; it is not nearly so difficult to ascribe temptation, *peirasmos*, to the action of God; it is much easier to see how temptation can lie within the providence of God.

We may now go on to look at the two clauses of this petition in detail.

First, there is the clause, Lead us not into temptation. All that we have said about the word *peirasmos* is true, and the early Christian writers were perfectly well aware of the facts, and yet in spite of it all there remains in the word *peirasmos* an overtone of evil. Always at the back of it there is the idea that a *peirasmos* in any sense of the word is something which is calculated to, or at least liable to, take a man's faith and loyalty away. The interpretations of this clause have therefore in one way or another sought to avoid the implication that God would ever deliberately do anything to attack or injure any man's faith.

Sometimes an escape road has been found by attaching special meanings to different words in the clause.

(i) A special stress has been laid upon the word *into*. *Into*, the Greek *eis*, could well stand for the Hebrew *lidhe*, which means *into the hands of*, and therefore *into the power of*. The meaning would then be something like this, if we put it into an amplified form: 'I know that temptation must come to me, for there can be no life without temptation. But, when it does come, as come it must, do not abandon me to it; do not deliver me helpless into its power; stand by me in my hour of need.' This would not be very different from Jesus' prayer for his disciples: 'I do not pray that thou shouldst take them out of the world, but that thou shouldst keep them from the evil one' (John 17.15). In that case this would not be so much an impossible prayer to be exempted from temptation as a prayer not to be abandoned helpless and unarmed to its attack and to its power. To put it positively, it would be a prayer for help when temptation comes.

(ii) Augustine has an interpretation of this clause much on the same lines. He draws a distinction (*The Sermon on the Mount* 2.9) between *being tempted* and being *brought into temptation*. All men must be tempted; but to be brought into temptation is to be brought into the power and the control of temptation; it is to be not only subjected to temptation but to be subdued by temptation.

Other writers have variations on this theme. In essence this interpretation takes the clause to be a prayer not for escape from temptation but for victory over temptation. Origen quotes the Greek version of Job 7.1 which says that all life is temptation, and then he goes on: 'Accordingly, let us pray to be delivered from temptation, not that we should not be tempted – which is impossible, especially for those on earth – but that we may not yield when we are tempted.... We should pray then not that we may not be tempted – which is impossible – but that we may not be brought under the power of temptation, which happens to them who are caught and captured by it' (*On Prayer* 29.9, 11). Origen quotes the example of Job. Job, he says, was delivered from temptation, not because the Devil did not attack him; the Devil in point of fact launched every kind of attack upon him; but because no matter what befell him he did not sin before the Lord, and showed himself to be just (*On Prayer* 30.1, 2). The deliverance lay not in the exemption from temptation but in the conquest of it. Luther took the same view. 'We cannot help', he said, 'being exposed to the assaults, but we pray that we may not fall and perish under them.'

Chrysostom goes even further. He takes the clause to mean, not only that we should not fall, but that we should not even enter into the struggle with temptation, lest we should fall. For him it is a prayer for the total elimination of temptation, but that is surely a prayer which cannot be answered within the human situation.

(iii) There is still a third line of interpretation, and this line was very common in the early Church. Augustine says that there were actually manuscripts of the New Testament in Latin in his day which rendered this clause: 'Do not allow us to be led into temptation.' (*Ne nos induci patiaris in temptationem*). This is in fact the interpretation of Tertullian, Cyprian and Augustine (Augustine, *Sermon on the Mount* 2.9; *On the Gift of Perseverance* 6; Tertullian, *On Prayer* 8; Cyprian, *The Lord's Prayer* 25).

It may well be that this is the correct interpretation. The Syriac version of the New Testament renders this clause: 'Do not *make us to enter into* temptations.' The Hebrew verb has a large variety of forms and this would go back to the Hebrew form of the verb known as the *Hiph'il*. The *Hiph'il* is the causative form of the verb, and means to make a person do something or other. Now this *hiph'il* form of the verb can be *permissive* as well as *causative*, and it can mean to *allow* a person to do something or other, and if in the original of the prayer a *hiph'il* was used by Jesus, it will mean: 'Do not allow us to enter into temptation', or: 'Do not allow us to be led into temptation.'

Here is an interpretation which gives us excellent sense, for in this case the meaning would be: 'Keep us from flirting with temptation. Keep us from situations in which temptation will get its chance. Defend us from the assaults of temptation which come from our own nature and from the seductions of others. Defend us from the attacks of the world, the flesh and the devil.' It would be a prayer that neither by our own weakness nor by the malice of others we may be brought into life situations in which we are foolishly and sometimes needlessly exposed to the attack of temptation. It would be a prayer in which we ask God to be the defender and the guardian of our faith, our loyalty and our purity.

These then are the main lines of interpretation of this clause, offered by those who hesitate to ascribe actual temptation to God, and certainly the last of them which turns the clause into a prayer for God's defending and preserving power is very attractive. But when all is said and done, there are two things to be said.

First, it is very doubtful if the Hebrew mind would have felt the difficulty of this clause. It is quite true that James says: 'Let no man when he is tempted say, I am tempted by God' (James 1.13), but, when we read the whole of the James passage, and when we see what is really in James' mind, we see that James is really condemning the man who puts the blame for his own sin upon God. He is thinking of the man who holds God to be responsible for his sin. But the whole bent of the Hebrew mind was to think that everything, literally everything, is in the hands of God and under his control. Because of this the Hebrew mind would have found no difficulty in believing that even temptation somehow fits into the plan and the purpose of God. Looking back over life Joseph said of his brothers: 'As for you, you meant evil against me; but God meant it for good' (Genesis 50.20). A Jew would not have found it difficult to believe that even apparent evil is woven into the pattern of God, since a Jew would have started out with the fundamental belief that nothing, literally nothing, can happen which is not the will of God.

Second, it may well be that in all our efforts at explanation we are allowing theological logic to take precedence over the natural human reaction of the heart.

To take a very simple human analogy and to put it in very simple and even colloquial terms, we can easily imagine a student saying to his teacher, or an athlete saying to his trainer, never doubting the love of the teacher or the good intent of the trainer: 'Go easy with me! Don't push me too hard!' It may well be that this is the best way in which to approach this petition; it may be best simply to see in it the instinctive appeal of the man who knows how weak he is and how dangerous life can be, and who takes his own peril to the protection of God. For the theologian the theological problem may be there; for the human being the theological problem is lost in the instinctive appeal of the human need.

There is the clause, Deliver us from evil. As we have seen, the translations in this clause are divided between, Deliver us from evil, in the general sense of the term, and, Deliver us from the Evil One in the sense of the Devil, the personal power of evil. The Greek can equally well mean either, and in point of fact the variation in translation makes very little difference to the meaning.

It is well to understand what the biblical writers understand by the Evil One. The Evil One goes under two names in the Bible.

(i) Sometimes he is called Satan. The word *satan* was not originally a proper name; it originally meant an *adversary* in the ordinary human sense of the term, and it is so used in Scripture seven times. The angel of the Lord is the adversary of Balaam, standing direct and opposing in his path (Numbers 22.22). Even when David appeared to throw in his lot with them, the Philistines fear that in battle he may turn out to be their adversary, their *satan* (1 Samuel 29.4). It is Solomon's thanksgiving that he has neither adversary (*satan*) nor misfortune (1 Kings 5.4). In later days both Hadad and Rezon are to become the *satans*, the adversaries, of Israel (1 Kings 11.14, 23, 25). A *satan* is simply an adversary.

Originally Satan was not an evil character; he was one of the sons of God (Job 1.6). But he had a special function. He was, so to speak, the prosecuting counsel against men; it was his function to say and to urge everything that could be said and urged against a man; he was man's adversary in the courts of God (Job 1.6–12): Satan is characteristically the Adversary of man.

(ii) Sometimes he is called the Devil. In Greek the word Devil is *diabolos*. *Diabolos* was originally neither a proper name nor a title. It is the normal Greek word for *slanderer*, and it is so used in the New Testament. Women in the Church must be serious minded and not *slanderers* (1 Timothy 3.11). In the last days *slanderers* (false accusers, AV) will arise (2 Timothy 3.3). The older women are not to be *slanderers* (false accusers) or slaves to drink (Titus 2.3).

So then the word *Satan* describes the Adversary who is the prosecuting counsel against men; the word Devil, *diabolos*, describes the one who is *par excellence*, the slanderer. And the two ideas are not so very different, because it is not so very far a cry from stating the case against a man to fabricating a case against a man. The aim of the Evil One is by any means to cause a breach between man and God, to break the relationship between man and God. The Evil One is the personification of all that is against God and all that is out to ruin man in this life and in the life to come.

It makes little difference whether we speak of evil or of the Evil One. We know quite well that there is in this world a force of evil which attacks goodness and which invites to sin. That force may be a personal force, or that force may be what we might call the cumulative effect of all the evil acts and evil decisions which have been part of the human scene. Be the force personal or impersonal, it is there. And this prayer is the prayer that we may be armoured and protected against it, and that we may be strengthened in our resistance power to it.

'The Lord', we read in the second Letter to Timothy, 'will rescue me from every evil and save us for his heavenly kingdom' (2 Timothy 4.18). And Luther puts the matter at its widest: 'In this prayer we ask our heavenly Father to set us free from all evil of body and soul, honour and estate: and finally, when our last hour comes, to vouchsafe us a happy end, and to take us from this valley of tears to himself in heaven.' As Luther sees it, this is the prayer for rescue in life and rescue in death.

Lead us not into temptation, but deliver us from evil. This concluding petition of the Lord's Prayer does three things. First, it frankly faces the danger of the human situation. Second, it freely confesses the inadequacy of human resources to deal with it. Thirdly, it takes both the danger and the weakness to the protecting power of God. And when we do all this we can say with Cyprian (*The Lord's Prayer* 27): 'When we have once asked for God's protection against evil and have obtained it, then against everything which the devil and the world can do against us, we stand secure and safe. For what fear is there in this life to the man whose Guardian in this life is God?'

# The Epilogue

The Lord's Prayer, as we commonly use it, has what we might
call its own built-in epilogue, for it ends with the ascription of
praise: 'For thine is the kingdom and the power and the glory, for
ever. Amen' (Matthew 6.13). As any of the newer translations will
show this was not part of the original prayer and it is not in the
earliest and the best manuscripts. Ultimately in the Church it
became part of the prayer because it was the response of the
congregation to the prayer. It is an ascription of praise with a
very long history, for it goes right back to the prayer of David,
when he was making the preparation for the Temple which his
son Solomon was one day to build: 'Thine, O Lord, is the greatness, and the power, and the glory, and the victory, and the
majesty; for all that is in the heaven and the earth is thine; thine
is the kingdom, O Lord, and thou art exalted as head above all'
(1 Chronicles 29.11). So, then, almost since men first began to
use the Lord's Prayer in public this has been the response of the
worshipping people to it.

The great value of this conclusion to the Lord's Prayer is that
it reminds us of two things. It reminds us to whom we have been
praying, and it reminds us that, if prayer is to be complete we
have to give as well as to take.

*Thine is the kingdom.* It may be that the word *kingdom* is mis-
leading here. To us kingdom tends to mean an area of land with
in which a king's rule is exercised. So we would speak of th
kingdom of Great Britain, meaning the country of Britain. B

here in the Lord's Prayer the word does not so much mean *kingdom* as it means *kingship*. The kingship is God's; his is the royal power; it is his right to exercise the power and the authority of king. Simply to say to God: 'Thine is the kingship; Thine is the royal power,' should be in itself an act of submission to God. We end the prayer by recognizing that God is king, that we are subjects, and by pledging our obedience and our allegiance to him.

*Thine is the power.* The word is *dunamis*, from which the English words *dynamic* and *dynamite* come. We end the prayer by reminding ourselves of the dynamic power of God. We end the prayer by thinking of the God in whom there is both the love to listen and the power to act. And, remembering that, we are bound to bring to God the trust and the confidence which his power demands. We end our prayer in the confidence that in his love God has heard, and that in his dynamic power he will answer.

*Thine is the glory.* The very word glory is a more than human word. We use the word loosely of the kind of honour and reputation and fame that some kind of human achievement can bring; but properly glory belongs to God alone. We end the prayer by reminding ourselves that we are in the presence of the divine glory; and that means that we must live life in the reverence which never forgets that it is living within the splendour of the glory of God.

And so, when we have prayed the Lord's Prayer, we rise from our knees and go out to the world and its ways remembering the royal sovereignty of God and pledged to obedience to him, remembering the dynamic power of God and trusting in that power to answer our prayers, remembering the glory of God and living with the reverence which knows that earth is penetrated and permeated with the divine glory.

## The Ten Commandments

The Ten Commandments are the fundamental law without which coherent society is impossible. They are principles of self-limitation and self-discipline which must be accepted by all people who wish to live together in any community.

They express the fundamental ethics common not only to Jewish and Christian ethical systems, but to *all* ethical systems. Jesus came into a society which already knew about goodness and morality, ethics and God. His teaching expanded the Jewish basis of ethics already established.

Dr Barclay, Professor of Divinity and Biblical Criticism at Glasgow University, draws on his knowledge of both Old and New Testaments to examine the way in which the Commandments demand reverence for God and respect for humankind, and reflect both the majesty of God and the rights of humans. He places great importance on the Commandments as a basic code of human conduct. This book is his way of communicating to the general reader what the scriptures have to say on the subject. He has always tried to bridge the gap between the academic and lay world, so the series is an important part of his theology.